The Best Life Ain't Easy But It's Worth It

For Joy,
Your love & wisdom
are all over these
pages! Thank you
for your deep friendship!
(Bookie (aka Virelle))

VIRELLE KIDDER

MOODY PUBLISHERS
CHICAGO

All Scripture quotations, unless otherwise indicated, are taken from the *Holy Bible, New International Version*®. NIV®. Copyright©1973, 1978, 1984 by International Bible Society. Used by permission of Zondervan. All rights reserved.

Scripture quotations marked KJV are taken from the King James Version.

Editor: Pam Pugh
Inside Design: Smartt Guys design
Cover Design: John Hamilton Design

Library of Congress Cataloging-in-Publication Data

Kidder, Virelle.
    The best life ain't easy : but it's worth it / Virelle Kidder.
        p. cm.
    Includes bibliographical references (p.).
    ISBN-13: 978-0-8024-4862-0
    1. Kidder, Virelle. 2. Christian biography—United States. I. Title.

BR1725.K475A3 2009
277.3'082092—dc22
[B]

                                                                    2008017583

We hope you enjoy this book from Moody Publishers. Our goal is to provide high-quality, thought-provoking books and products that connect truth to your real needs and challenges. For more information on other books and products written and produced from a biblical perspective, go to www.moodypublishers.com or write to:

Moody Publishers
820 N. LaSalle Boulevard
Chicago, IL 60610

1 3 5 7 9 10 8 6 4 2

Printed in the United States of America

To my dear children:

Lauren Elizabeth Kidder McGarry
Amy Lynn Kidder
David Steven Kidder
and
Robert Edward Tonkin Kidder

Next to being your dad's girlfriend,
being your mom is the best part of my life.
I love you!

Contents

Foreword

It's important to share an oral and written history with your family, the events that unfurl in layers of love, tension, risks, brokenness, and redemption that create a family. That's why this book is a gift—as much a gift to my family as it can be to yours.

I have the luxury of knowing many of the people in the enclosed stories. *The Best Life Ain't Easy* is a moving and complete record of my mother's faith experience—the loss of a father, a young longing for God, the relationship between a widow and her daughter, the meeting of the noble man of my father, the complexity and uncertainty of raising four children, and twisting paths of physical and psychological health. Most importantly, it's a joyful story about conversion, and the resulting lifetime commitment of significant obedience, listening, renewal, and achievement for God.

Likely, you've walked some, or many of the same roads described in this book. You may have experienced more highs, or more lows, but the central theme of this book—Returning to Love—will not be lost on you. Of all the traits I admire most in my mother, one stands out above all others: transparency. The idea of being "known" is fraught with complexities that demand a greater reliance and obedience on God, an extraordinary belief in, and extension of, undeserved forgiveness—grace given to others. The idea of transparency many be the most daring thesis in this book, because it requires that we deliberately love: not simple easy love, but hard love. The kind of love God demands from us: selfless, unconditional, reflective, obedient love.

It is my hope when you close the last page of this book, you can't help but commit to the central, daring idea that is embedded throughout this book: It never easy to Return to Love, but it has the greatest reward. Put in motion, the permanent choice to love keeps marriages, families, and children together, and weaves a story worthy of a book.

DAVID S. KIDDER, two-time *New York Times* bestselling author

Stopped on the

Way to the Fair

When I was six years old and my brother Roger was ten, my father piled the four of us into our '51 maroon and gray Dodge and headed to the Thousand Islands on the St. Lawrence River. To this day, I remember being carsick in the backseat from both parents smoking in the front. Roger entertained me for hours with funny word games and whispered jokes. No one wanted to make Daddy mad.

On the way home, we stopped for lunch in a pretty, small town named Mexico in upstate New York, a few miles from Lake Ontario. Driving down Main Street, we passed an impressive brick school with huge white pillars, which had a bubbling stream running alongside it. Lush maple trees lined the streets, shading quaint Victorian homes and spired churches. The downtown was small but adequate with a post office, an old-fashioned A & P, a barbershop, a dry goods store, a bakery, and a shoemaker.

My father fell in love on the spot. Right after lunch he located a realtor and bought a six-room, 150-year-old gray house on Lincoln

Avenue at the edge of town. He had no job there; we had neither relatives nor friends. But no one protested, not even my mother. Moving was an annual event in our family. I thought everybody did it.

The day the big van unloaded our things, I met my best friend, Barbie. Her sister Jane rode around the corner on her bike and invited me home for lunch. Both sisters had cute Buster Brown haircuts with bangs. Barb was shorter than me and shy, but full of adventure. Soon we were inseparable.

At home Mother papered and painted every room. Daddy had the house painted red, built a white fence around it himself in the hot sun, and planted hollyhocks, purple iris, and climbing roses. He never worked again in the yard, but often sat alone admiring his work from a lawn chair in our side yard.

That summer he also joined AA. Dr. Thompson, an anesthetist from Syracuse, became his sponsor. The Thompsons often visited us, bringing along their two champion black Newfoundlands, Sam and Mary, in the back of their station wagon. Sam would lay on the car horn with one enormous paw until Dr. Thompson would let them out for a walk around our yard. I loved those dogs. I especially enjoyed tightly gripping their leashes while they dragged me down the gravel driveway, and I'd laugh until I wet my pants. The dogs even came to the AA picnics and Dr. Thompson would show off their tricks for the crowd. My father and mother looked happy again. We all relaxed a bit.

Sometimes I sat and talked with my father in the yard, asking him to tell me funny stories. Telling stories was his favorite thing. I brought Barbie and Jane to meet him one day, hoping he'd entertain them, too, but he didn't feel like being funny that day.

One day my father brought home a baby blue parakeet. Roger and I named him Herbie. Daddy spent hours talking to that bird and training it on the dining room table. "Put your finger out and let him sit on it," he coaxed us. "He won't hurt you." And he didn't. Roger and I had parakeets for years after that, way into our adult lives. My father's patience with pets was limitless. People were another matter.

By the time I was seven, I knew Daddy was mentally ill, besides being an alcoholic. I'm fairly certain he loved us, but his temper was frightening and unpredictable. No one dared upset him. We were his second try at family life. I learned years later through legal papers that came in the mail, that an earlier wife and two sons remained in his wake just as we would. I longed to know them and often wondered where they were.

About the time our little red house in Mexico was painted and pretty, my father left. He spent his last night with us awake, smoking in his overstuffed chair in the living room, watching our bedroom doors. Many years later Mother told me she had lain awake all night in fear. In the morning, Roger and I walked to school. When we came home, he was gone.

I found Mother washing dishes. She never looked up when I asked, "Where's Daddy?"

"He left." *Is she crying?* I wondered.

"When is he coming back?"

"He's not." *Why isn't she crying?*

"Where did he go?" *Maybe I can run after him and bring him home!*

"I don't know."

The conversation was clearly over. I never asked again, but I cried in my bed at night begging God to tell me where he was. I couldn't think of anyone outside our family to ask. We had secrets. Talking about Daddy was soon forbidden. There was no one left to ask but God, and I barely knew Him at all. I remember thinking, *maybe a Bible would help.*

No one spoke about Daddy again. It was easier that way for my mother, who suffered silently most of the time. The next fall she went back to teaching school. We all tried to act normal. Roger played basketball, did the lawn, and took out the garbage. I rode my bike, played with Barbie, and helped in small ways like dusting and wiping dishes. Life was quiet, predictable, and safe for the first time I could remember. Mother tried hard to make life good for us. She sewed clothing, made birthday parties, and gave us big Christmases she couldn't afford. Her light was always on when I went to sleep. She'd work until late at night correcting papers. Roger and I both tried to be good and, we hoped, were making her happy. For me, it became a lifetime yoke.

Most of my growing up was spent with Barbie, hanging upside down in trees, or playing cowgirls wearing my favorite six-shooters in the woods, picking blackberries, or building forts and pretend campfires. We knew every trail in the two-acre woods behind my house clear through to the hilly backyards of Church Street. It was our happy kingdom. Barb's family eventually moved to a farm outside of town. We saw each other less often, but remained best friends for years. When she wasn't around, I made a pest of myself with Roger and his friends until he'd beg Mother to call me inside or do something with me.

Life could get very boring around our house. Rainy days were especially lonely. I'd stay in my room and play paper dolls or store, or sweep off the red Congoleum rug in our stone basement, arranging porch furniture and pretending it was my home, the one I'd like to live in one day. I folded napkins into triangles and welcomed neighborhood kids as guests for crackers and cherry Kool-Aid.

My imagination became a retreat into a more interesting world. It probably saved my life. As I grew, my imagination almost took over. By the time I was ten, it was getting me in trouble. I exaggerated nearly everything, only I called it storytelling. I liked it that way. Real life was dull and full of things we weren't allowed to talk about, like where babies came from, and what was the meaning of life, and where my father was.

Then, in fifth grade something amazing happened—a district-wide short story contest. My teacher, Mrs. Bullock, insisted I enter it. When she mentioned the first prize was any book you wanted, I knew I wanted a Bible. Instantly, I had a story in mind about a young boy my age who loved his horse, but the horse ran away. He searched and searched for the horse. It became a chapter book complete with drawings. Of course, the horse was found, and the boy was jubilant. I had no idea I was really writing about my father. I won first prize, and eventually took home a big red Bible.

"Why did you want that?" My mother couldn't hide her disappointment. "Why not some good book like *Honeybunch* or *The Bobbsey Twins*?"

"I just wanted it, that's all," I said, tucking it under my arm and disappearing into my bedroom. Sitting on the corner of my bed, I opened it gently and caressed the new pages. *The answers to life are in here.* It was a holy moment.

But where to read? *I'll start at the beginning!* I read a few paragraphs, but nothing made sense. Not in the middle, either, not even in the familiar chapters called, "Matthew," "Mark," "Luke," or "John." I slammed it closed. *I can't believe it! There's nothing here! No answers at all! It's a lie! God must be a hoax just like the Easter Bunny and Santa!* Waves of acute disappointment turned to tears. I felt completely alone.

Two years later, Mother woke me for school one bright April morning. In the same voice she'd use to tell me breakfast was ready, she said, "Your father died last night. He had a heart attack. His landlady called. You're not to tell anyone about this at school. Only Aunt Char knows."

I sat up straight. "Does Roger know?"

"Yes." I ran quickly to his room and found him still in his pajamas reading a book in bed.

"Don't you know Daddy died?" I asked, stunned by the casualness of the news.

"Yes." He barely looked up.

"Don't you care?"

"No. Not really." It was years before I would know of the verbal and physical abuse Roger had endured. For now, I turned away to process my father's death alone. I learned that grief couldn't be buried as easily as the dead. Like snakes under the porch, grief and unanswered questions can live underneath your life and frighten you a long, long time.

I never quite forgot my father or God, but I tried. Both I considered out of my life, less relevant with time, subjects best not talked about. Mother was right. It was easier that way. I moved on to enjoy high school academics, a mix of achievements, music, and fun with my friends. Barbie had retreated into her own world by that time. We saw little of one another in the years that followed, choosing colleges a hundred miles apart. I applied at only one school, the University at Albany in the capital, and chose a double major in Spanish and English. At nineteen, college friends invited me to spend an exciting summer studying in Spain where I found life far more colorful than any of my early imaginings.

Strangely, I still felt agonizingly lonely at times. Friends were, after all, only friends. They only cared about you so much. My mother and brother were busy with their own lives. I wanted more. I began to want a man—not just a man; I wanted a prince. Impossible. They didn't really exist. I decided to pray for one.

Pray? Where did that idea come from? How did anyone really believe in that? God simply didn't answer. I doubted He was even real. *Still . . .*

I began praying silently on my mile-long walk to class. *Lord, if You're real, show me by three o'clock.* At 3:01 I'd check my watch. Nothing. I felt like a fool. Surely, He could have found some way to let me know. I prayed the same prayer again the next day, and the next, trying to give God a chance to prove Himself to me. Day after day, 3:01 would come, and nothing happened. I didn't need a Salvation Army band, just some small sign. I stretched the deadline to four o'clock. Nothing. Then, anytime this week.

I became preoccupied with God, haunted by His silence. I told no one. Only God knew, if He was even real. Seeking Him became my obsession. Months passed. Then, at 10:00 a.m. one day in late spring, Steve Kidder walked into Dr. Creegan's philosophy class and sat down right in front of me.

He was late, too.

The dark green leather jacket he wore that day still hangs in our closet. The English boots are gone, as is his dark hair. But the prince remains. I loved him the moment I saw him. The greater miracle was that he loved me, too.

Life became a romance—days whirled into months and the music lasted. It lasted through college, through our first years of marriage, through a new baby and grad school, through Steve's first job at Johns Hopkins as a new PhD, right up until that hot Sunday in Baltimore when our new friends Ginny and Keith invited us to church and home for dinner. It lasted until the moment Keith opened his Bible and asked if he could read a psalm, and I saw Steve stiffen in his chair next to me, and felt my throat tighten with some choking, buried anger. Until the moment after Keith read aloud and I said, "May I ask you something?" That was the moment the music began to die.

I hardly noticed it go. I was consumed once again with knowing God. Tearing through the boxes in our basement, I unearthed the mildewed Bible I'd won in fifth grade. I read it all summer, barely noticing Steve, or the joy leaving him. You could hardly hear the music anymore.

I took a new lover that fall. His name was Jesus. He was all I ever wanted, the God I'd hungered for so long. How could loving Him not be right? I hung on His words, talked of Him day and night, lived and breathed His Word, and gave myself to Him with abandon.

I barely looked at Steve except to notice his lack of interest in my new faith. I seldom looked in the mirror, for that matter, to see how plain I'd become. Steve didn't understand me now. He wanted the old me back. He wanted the music again. How could I tell him I'd given it away?

CHAPTER 2

Wake Me When
the Fun Begins

"Want to come?" I asked flatly, knowing what the answer would be.

"No, I'll stay home."

I stared at my unshaven husband. Steve had as much interest in my new faith as he did in learning to sew. I tried every tactic to change his mind: arguments, manipulation, even pleading. Nothing worked.

"I figured that."

"I'm just not interested in going to church again," Steve said. "It's not for me. You go if you like, but I'm staying home and watching a game on TV." With that, he settled down on the long blue sofa, put his feet on the coffee table, and leaned back.

Three-year-old Lauren bounced down the stairs, her long blonde pigtails flying out to the side like wings. "Are you coming to church with us, Daddy?" She was his soft spot, but even Lauren's cute voice wasn't working.

"No, honey," I answered for him. "Daddy's busy."

"He doesn't look busy. Why aren't you coming, Daddy?"

Steve looked daggers at me.

"We'll talk about this later. Better leave, girls."

I felt like slamming the door, and would have, if Lauren hadn't been there. I was disgusted to the core with my husband. He even refused to hear about God anymore. Ever since my mother had flown down from Albany to find out where I'd parked my brains, and my brother arrived shortly afterward from Cincinnati (certainly at her request) to "straighten me out," Steve had allies. He wasn't going to budge.

In a few short months since my radical choice to commit my life to Christ, our happiness quotient had plummeted from a ten to a two. We were both miserable; the tension in our marriage was getting hard to hide. If only he'd believe.

Fine! I thought. *God may have other plans for me, anyway! Maybe I'll be a missionary someplace. I already speak Spanish. Lauren and I could live in another country.* But the martyr approach didn't last. I was too mad.

Twenty minutes later, Lauren and I arrived at church and made our way to the second row on the left, smiling at friends along the aisle. I loved these people. They were my family now. I knew they often felt sorry for us sitting alone without Steve, or at least I thought they did.

While Lauren wiggled in the pew and colored on the program as she waited for children's church to begin, I fingered my red Bible and thought of the deepening rift in our marriage. If Steve really loved me, why wouldn't he love the same God I do now? It would make us happy again. Why was he acting so stubborn and belligerent? I glanced around the sanctuary at other couples who looked so happy. Most of the husbands sat with an arm around their wife, looking snug and in love. Where was my husband? At home watching a game on television.

In only a few short months, our love had grown cold. We didn't laugh at the same things, enjoy the same activities, or like the same friends now. Steve was suspicious of my Christian friends, feeling like a target for Evangelism Explosion. Television shows we once enjoyed now had little appeal for me. I preferred reading my Bible. Beyond matters of faith, raising Lauren sparked our biggest clashes. Steve was a "softy," leaving me as the heavy every time, one more thing that widened the gap between us. Intimacy, once a delight, now languished into awkward, lonely moments in bed together. I often turned toward the wall and cried silently to sleep.

God, what do You expect from me now? This isn't what I thought would happen! What if Steve never comes to Christ? How long can we last like this? For the first time, other women's husbands looked good to me. Too good. I wanted one like they had.

Often at night Lauren wanted her Daddy to tuck her in. Naturally, she stacked up five or six books on his lap, all Bible stories. Steve was cornered by his love for her, staying up in her room a long time talking, reading, and listening to her prayers. One night, when he finally came down, he was fuming.

"All she wants me to read are Bible stories now. I read them, and then she asks me, 'Do you believe that, Daddy?' What am I supposed to say? You've been filling her head with all this Bible stuff. It's too much!"

I sat on the couch, acting calm, reading my Bible again. "How can it be too much?"

"That's all she's getting is your side of the story! I'm going to tell her mine!"

"And what *is* yours?" I responded in a snippy voice. "Or don't you know?" With that, he turned abruptly and went back upstairs. Another happy evening off to a great start.

A couple of weeks later, Steve came home from work in a little brighter mood. "Want to come to our Christmas party at the research center?" he asked.

"Of course I want to come. Why wouldn't I?" Who wouldn't want to go to a catered party at the gorgeous English Tudor carriage house Johns Hopkins used for educational research? With its big fireplaces and leather furniture, it would be decorated to the hilt. We'd get dressed up for a change.

"There will be a lot of people you don't know and a lot of drinking."

"Oh." I had been hanging around Christians exclusively for three months. Could I still enjoy an evening out with the worldly, intellectual crowd Steve spent his time with? But Keith and Ginny would probably be there since Keith and Steve worked together. I'd spend time with them. If they could do it, I could, too. "Okay. I'll come," I said, knowing I probably wouldn't enjoy myself at all.

We tucked Lauren in with a neighborhood babysitter and drove silently to the research center. I looked my best that night in a new white wool two-piece dress with fake fur trim, patent leather heels, extra makeup, and my favorite jewelry. Steve looked handsome as always in a dark suit and red tie.

The place was packed with twenty- and thirty-somethings in holiday garb. A giant Christmas tree sparkled in the large paned windows; candles, music, and a fire roaring on the hearth made it picture perfect. The mood was loud and happy, fueled with yuletide spirits. We made the rounds meeting and greeting people. Steve introduced me to many of his coworkers. To my disappointment, Keith and Ginny hadn't arrived yet. While Steve talked research with his friends, I headed straight for the kitchen and offered to help with the food. It seemed a comfortable place at the time.

"Hi, I'm Vickie," a cute blonde in a slinky black cocktail dress said, smiling broadly at me. I'd just opened my mouth to respond when she handed me an oven mitt adding, "Say, do you want to watch these hors d'oeuvres for me? They only need ten minutes in the oven. There's a tray over there. I'll be right back."

I stood like a police guard in front of the oven, smiling at a roomful of people I didn't know. *Hmm. Maybe I should wear the oven mitt so they'll know why I'm here.* They were all too engaged in conversation to smile back. I stood at my post wondering when Keith and Ginny would show up. Where was Steve, anyway? Soon I began to eavesdrop on a conversation a few feet away. The loudest voice came from a tall, good-looking Englishman with a shock of blond hair that kept falling in his eyes. He wore a tan sweater and jeans.

"Of course, it's only a bloody commercial holiday. Nobody believes in Christmas anymore! That's if they've got half a brain! They'd get laughed out of Oxford." How clever of him. Admiring chuckles rolled from his audience's lips. *He's making fun of my Savior! Am I going to stand here and not defend Him?* I sincerely wished I'd stayed home, but this was my first opportunity to stand up publicly for Christ. I put my hat in the ring.

"What do you mean by that? Do you think Christ's birth never happened?"

Silence. One by one, people stopped talking and laughing. They turned to look at me, a small white-clad policeman wearing an oven mitt.

"Of course it never happened." It was the blonde and I, facing off. My face burned hot. I felt like the whole universe waited for my response.

"I believe Jesus is real, that He was actually born on this earth. Christmas is real. It's not a joke."

"Let me ask you something." The Brit leveled his gaze at me. "Do you have eternal life?"

I wanted to run. *Oh, God, help me not fail You!* "Yes," I answered.

His tone was loud and insulting. "Then I would consider you the same as a member of the Flat-Earth Society."

No one spoke. The crowd of listeners turned and left the kitchen quietly, including the blond young atheist, chuckling to himself.

I'd never been so grateful for an oven mitt.

Normally, I'd have wanted to find Steve and go home, crying all the way there. But I didn't. I turned toward the oven to hide my tears, opened the door and removed a tray of perfectly baked hors d'oeuvres. As the aroma filled the air, another Voice whispered in my ear, *I'm proud of you, Child. I'm so proud of you.*

I took a deep breath and let it out slowly. Being a Christian was not going to be easy. I knew that. But if that was the worst thing anyone could dish out, I'd made it through my first acid test. God was pleased, and I was really His child. Maybe Steve and I would make it after all.

I arranged the platter of hot pigs-in-a-blanket, swung out of the kitchen, held them high, and smiled at the whole roomful of strangers. Steve caught my eye and looked surprised to see me look happy.

"Hot hors d'oeuvres, anyone? Right out of the oven."

CHAPTER 3

Paddling Upstream

The Christmas season carried us on a hopeful tide. Things warmed up between us as we shopped for gifts and baked cookies. Friends from church invited us to chop down our Christmas trees together in the snowy mountains of western Maryland. With three happy little girls between us giggling and singing carols in the car, we drove up a snowy rough road to the Christmas tree farm. Leaving our cars parked, we trudged through the snow until we found two perfect trees and sawed them down. Unfortunately, finding our cars again was not so easy, as the late afternoon sun set quickly behind the next ridge, leaving us in total darkness dragging around two enormous Christmas trees.

Steve's years of experience in the woods eventually led us in the right direction, and soon we were inching down the mountain, headed toward a hamburger place on the main road. It was the first time in a long time I'd seen Steve enjoy himself.

Life was going to be good again. I just knew it. But there was more good news on the way.

Part of the tension between us was entirely out of our control. We'd wanted another baby for a long time. Two months earlier I had thought I might be pregnant. But when I visited the OB/GYN, he had confirmed that not only was I not pregnant, but that I had severe endometriosis, which gave me a 90 percent chance of never conceiving again. "Keep trying to get pregnant, if you like," the doctor said, "but you're probably sterile." It was a crushing blow.

We both wanted more children, but Steve especially didn't handle this development well at all. Coming from a family of six highly charged kids, raising Lauren as an only child seemed unthinkable. He became bitter about it right away. "So this is how God treats you now? Doesn't seem too nice to me!"

I have no idea why, other than grace, but God kept me calm. I felt His urging to just trust Him and wait. We'd put our names in for adoption with the county, knowing the wait would be long.

And then, two days before Christmas, a simple urine test confirmed I was pregnant. Steve was beyond elated. Hope surged inside me.

A happy Christmas came and went. In the new year, relieved to be pregnant, I redoubled my efforts to do everything right. I volunteered to help with Mrs. Foley's Good News Club, an outreach ministry to neighborhood kids through which Lauren was led to Christ the next year. I went to Wednesday night prayer meetings at church, always mentioning Steve's need for salvation; I joined a Scripture memory group rehearsing a new Bible verse over and over every day. About a dozen young couples from church invited us to join their monthly Bible study. In spite of the fact that he only came because I dragged him there, Steve grew to care deeply for every one of them, although he sensed he was their pet prayer project and hated that. Once every month I attended Christian Women's Club dinners at a nearby restaurant, inviting friends and neighbors.

But Steve remained unchanged. What was I thinking? That I could impress God with my spiritual activity? Did I think He would answer my prayers for Steve in proportion to how much I proved myself to Him? How little I really knew God then, as if studying more, serving more, praying more, even begging more would make Him respond more. I was changing nothing except our marriage. That was rapidly approaching ground zero. Again. If anything, Steve distanced himself even more from God and from me. Today I wish I could reach back and slap myself for being such a fool.

Into this strange mix, our miracle baby arrived. After a long summer pregnancy, much of it spent drinking ice tea with my feet on a pillow, beautiful dark-haired Amy Lynn was born in late July. Steve marveled at her long slender fingers, dark curly hair, and gorgeous features. "She's Miss America," he announced as Keith and Ginny admired the wiggling pink newborn on our bed.

Knowing Steve's background in biology and evolution, Keith quipped, "Just think, Steve, she could have been a toad!" I worried how Steve would respond, but he laughed it off good-naturedly. *Steve must know this baby is a gift from God! Why doesn't he see that?*

Two kids kept life busier than ever. Amy was consistently a sleeper, a giggler, or a screamer. Lauren, an adoring big sister at four, became her live-in slave, learning early how to turn Amy's screams into shrieks of laughter with puppet shows, dancing, songs, and acrobatics. Because of the Baltimore heat, we soon moved Amy's crib into Lauren's air-conditioned bedroom, where the laughter never stopped, and Lauren learned to sleep through anything, which was a very good thing.

Tensions grew daily between Steve and me, but neither of us liked aised voices. Since Steve's parents never fought in front of [chil]dren, and I'd learned early that unleashed anger could be dangerous, we resorted to late night discussions that ruined every evening. I'd start it off with my familiar plea. "I wish you'd read this book, Steve. I think it would help you." Sometimes I was blatantly rude. "I don't see how you can sit there and watch TV. Maybe if you read your Bible once in a while and gave it some thought, you'd see your need for Christ."

He'd look the other way and sigh, or close his eyes like he was dying inside. "Maybe I just don't want to, okay? Can't you love me like I am?"

Great! How long am I going to have to do that?

Steve was often angry, but never blew up at me or stormed out of the house. In spite of these divisions, we both wanted our marriage to survive. The problem was, neither of us wanted it enough to change—until one Sunday the following spring.

It was a hot day, and Lauren and I had just come home from church. Steve had stayed home while Amy napped. Now he was hungry.

"What's for lunch?" he mumbled, barely looking up from the couch. There he sat, unshaven, still in his bathrobe, watching a ball game on TV. He looked just as bad as he had two hours earlier when we left. I was not happy. Out to the kitchen I went, and with a loud banging of pots and pans, slapped together a colorless meal.

We sat down like inmates and I said a stiff prayer over dinner. Steve looked up and asked, "How was church?"

"It was wonderful," I returned flatly. "You might have liked it if you'd been there." I shot him a disapproving glance.

"I don't think so. I don't fit in there," he answered thoughtfully, and after a long pause added, "You know, if I were you, I'd feel guilty."

"Guilty? Guilty?" I exploded, bringing my fist down hard on the table. Lauren darted out of the room. "Why should I feel guilty? You're the one who's rejected Christ! You're the one who refuses to believe! How do you have the nerve to say that?"

And with the softest words I ever heard, Steve directed his blue-green eyes at mine and delivered a blow I would never recover from. "Because, Virelle, I am a pagan, and I'm behaving exactly like a pagan should behave, but you are a Christian, and you are not loving." For once, I had no words.

As soon as I'd cleared the lunch dishes, I marched upstairs to have a talk with God. Steve went back to his ball game. I locked our bedroom door and got down on my knees. *Lord, You know Steve can't possibly be right, don't You? You know how hard I've tried to grow as a Christian. I've done everything, Lord. You don't think I'm unloving, too, do You?* Silence. In an instant, I realized God agreed with Steve.

This was bad news. I had to change, and radically at that. I had no idea where to begin. That's when tears came. Torrents of them. I cried and prayed about an hour, begging God to forgive me. I'd made such a mess of my marriage, our family life, even my performance-based faith. How would I ever start over now?

Then came a new thought, entirely foreign to my own. I sensed God wanted me to love Steve as if he were already the man I prayed he would become, whether it happened now, or in thirty years, or sometime after my death. If faith really was "being sure of what we hope for and certain of what we do not see," (Hebrews 11:1), I had to believe God would answer my deepest prayers for Steve in His own way, in His own time. Tough terms, but I wasn't exactly in a bargaining position. I agreed, though fairly certain I'd never live long enough to see the answer.

A whisper came. *Why don't you ask Steve's forgiveness?*

Do I have to, Lord? He'll laugh at me. He'll never believe me! Isn't there some other way?

Apparently not. I went downstairs trembling. Steve looked up briefly. He was obviously not thrilled to see me.

"I came down to ask your forgiveness."

"Oh, yeah? That's nice."

"I really mean it. You were right. I've been very critical and unloving. Please forgive me. I'll stop." *What a lame confession! He'll think it's a ploy, another setup.*

I can't remember if anything else was said. Probably not much. I felt like a complete failure as a wife and a Christian. There was no way to throw in the towel and no place to throw it. I'd have to change, but how?

The hardest part was over: agreeing with God that I'd blown it. I was a pain to live with and I knew it. Being honest, I asked myself if I'd want to come home to the complainer I'd become. I asked God to show me how to become a loving wife, if I was even capable of being one.

Changing came in small steps. First, I put away all the tracts and Christian books I'd planted about the house. No more reading my Bible in front of him or asking him to attend church, either. That meant setting him up with church friends was out, too. It felt like condemning myself to loneliness. *God, did I understand You right? Stop me if I'm going too far with this, okay?* I didn't hear "stop."

Instead, I started all over again learning to smile and say, "Good morning," while bringing Steve his coffee while he shaved. Making his favorite cookies was my next idea, but what were they? I had forgotten. I had a long road ahead of me. Loving Steve without preaching at him or registering my disapproval at every little "mistake" he made meant doing the hard work of forgiveness. When my resolve began to fade and I'd get huffy or preachy again, I'd wear a path to a quiet corner of my kitchen and ask God's help.

I realized one day that, although I couldn't change Steve's hostility toward my new faith, I could learn better ways of handling it. Occasionally he would grumble about Lauren and me attending church, and I would offer to stay home. A few times he tested my sincerity by taking me up on it. Then, I needed a serious attitude adjustment in a hurry, but God didn't let me down.

But words were, frankly, my biggest problem. I had far too many of them. It was a rude awakening for me when I realized God didn't need my mouth to teach Steve anything. In fact, He did much better without me. One morning Proverbs 12:18 warned me, "Reckless words pierce like a sword, but the tongue of the wise brings healing." I desperately needed a transfusion of healing words.

It got harder still.

My Christian friends urged me to do more than just give up being Steve's chief critic; they urged me to get on his team, learn to put his plans and interests ahead of my own, and look for every opportunity to help him shine. I watched how they did it. They listened more to their husband's challenges and joys at work, wore a pleasant facial expression, discussed solutions for the day's dilemmas rather than dumping them on each other at dinner. They looked for things to laugh about and created beauty in the little things that make up life. And they prayed hard for every detail that touched his life.

Could I do that? I could try.

I asked God to guide Steve with His hand on his shoulder all day long, to give him wisdom and protection, and to open the right doors in his life and close the rest. Then, I had to believe that God was doing it, even if Steve wasn't yet the spiritual leader I longed for. And God knocked my socks off with His answers.

When our car, for example, suddenly gave up the ghost, Steve's stress meter went off the scale. I prayed like mad for a miracle. Within a few days a car dealer from our church offered us a free loaner car while we shopped for another. I marvel now at the man's patience. He soon found us one of the most beautiful cars we've ever owned and sold it to us at a price even we could afford on a squeaky budget. Steve was amazed, and I leaped for joy inside.

Around this time I met Elizabeth, one of the most beautiful women I had ever met. Silver-haired and sixtyish, Elizabeth radiated stylish poise and unflappable acceptance of others. Her husband, Fred, was a quiet man, likable but not much for socializing. Whenever he came to church, they amazed me by often holding hands, and I'd think to myself, *That's the kind of marriage I wish we could have someday.*

It wasn't long before Elizabeth included me as a helper in her weekly ministry to neighborhood children, something clearly close to her heart. Her lovely voice made Bible stories come alive each week for a room full of squirmy kids, including my four-year-old daughter. One day I confided my deep loneliness at home and the terrible longing I felt for Steve to share my faith.

"I know how you feel, Virelle," she answered, leveling those beautiful gray-blue eyes at me. "I've been praying for Fred for forty years."

"What?" I blurted out my amazement. "How have you lasted this long? How come you both seem so happy?"

"I learned one day that God called me to love Fred, to honor him, and make his life as happy as I possibly could. He never asked me to change him. Only someone as big and powerful as God can change a husband! In spite of Fred not sharing my faith, we've found a happy life together and God has done wonderful things in our children's lives. They are all strong believers and pray every day for their dad. I have no doubt that God will honor those prayers." And He did. I learned many years later that Fred received Christ as Savior shortly before his death.

What made Elizabeth so beautiful? It had to be her loving heart, one that ruled her tongue, her facial expressions, her voice, her touch, her time. She was the evidence I needed, the perfect visual of a Christ-filled life. I wanted to become like that, no matter what it took.[1]

Note

1. Portions of this chapter are adapted from an article that first appeared in *Today's Christian Woman* (May/June 1998) as "When He Doesn't Believe."

CHAPTER 4

Tasting Love
for the First Time

Learning to love Steve again meant sheer obedience. I seldom felt like it. When an older friend named Vernon from church invited him to go fishing on Saturdays on the Chesapeake Bay in his magnificent boat, my plans for family fun or projects around the house went down the drain.

"Do you mind if I go?" he asked, looking like Christmas had arrived early.

"I guess it's okay. Just leave the car keys." *Like I have somewhere to go with two kids.*

"Thanks! I'll do whatever you want around the house when I get back. Go ahead and eat without me. Vernon said something about getting steaks on the way home."

"Sure. Have fun." I faked a smile and waved good-bye.

Saturdays took a lot of attitude adjustment on my part. I'd start off whining at God. *Lord, there went my plans! Now, what am I supposed to do?*

"Hey, Mommy, can we bake something?" Lauren, now five, could sense an opening. She loved making cookies together. She even named her favorite doll "Cookie."

Why not? "What shall we bake, honey?"

"How about something for Daddy? He loves oatmeal cookies!" She was already dragging a stool over to the counter. How could I say no?

"Okay, honey. Let me grab our aprons." *Someone* else was behind this, I just knew it.

Soon we'd be elbow deep in flour and sugar, Lauren with her little bowl of ingredients, and me with the big one. As Lauren chattered away and sang songs, Amy napped or sat in her wind-up swing. The kitchen soon smelled delicious with hot cookies cooling on paper grocery bags all over the counter.

"Daddy's going to love these!" Lauren grinned as she spooned raw oats into her mouth, which was now ringed with flour.

"You're right, honey! Want some hot cookies and milk now?" I didn't need to ask.

Those were the good Saturdays. There were others.

One of the worst tests happened on one of their fishing days. The Ringling Brothers' Barnum & Bailey Circus was in town. I'd always wanted to go, since my middle name is Barnum. (I have no idea if this is true, but our family is supposedly among P. T. Barnum's last living relatives.) I bought tickets for Saturday afternoon and arranged for a babysitter for Amy. Steve promised to be home from fishing in time.

Lauren and I were beyond excited and ready early, but no Steve. An hour went by, and we watched for him from the upstairs bedroom window. After two hours, we were convinced Daddy had been in an accident. Lauren and I prayed fervently. "Oh, Lord, please keep Daddy safe and bring him home. Protect him, Lord, and don't let anything bad happen to him."

Another hour passed and we forgot all about our prayers. Lauren was draped over the upstairs windowsill, crying with disappointment. I sat on our bed angrily rehearsing what I would say the moment he walked in the door. I was seething.

Long after the circus must have ended, Steve and Vernon pulled up to the curb out front. Steve told me later he's never been so afraid to come in the door. They'd been contriving excuses all the way home.

"There he is, Mommy!" Lauren cried out. I descended the stairs, ready to fire all six barrels of well-thought-out comments.

When I was halfway down the stairs, I heard a little whisper: *Why not show him grace instead of anger?* I melted. As Steve stepped into the house, I found myself wrapping him in a huge hug.

"I'm so sorry," he began. "We lost track of time. I'm really sorry about the circus."

"It's okay, honey. We can go tomorrow." *Where did that come from?*

Quite honestly, it was like an out-of-body experience. Lauren sat on the stairs watching in disbelief.

Events like these happened more often in our home, softening our relationship over time. God's grace was more powerful than I realized, available any time I needed it. And I needed it a lot.

With each small victory over selfishness and anger, mutual trust returned between us. Gradually, we relaxed again little by little, and learned to ask each other before making plans. Steve tried, too. He began bringing me coffee, cleaning up the kitchen, and helping with laundry. He acted happy again, and so did I. Laughter came back, as did spontaneity and humor. We held hands, snuggled on the couch, and enjoyed being a couple again. Love came back in a flood, unencumbered by our earlier self-interest, and with it, the music we'd thought lost. Better music this time. For the first time in a long time, our marriage brought deep satisfaction and joy.

Now that I wasn't on his case all the time, Steve began to explore his questions about faith. Occasionally he'd come to church, and secretly bought a paperback Bible at Kmart, reading at work on his lunch break. He still refused to talk about God with me, which was frustrating. I tried to wait and thank God for what I couldn't yet see.

The next spring God began to tighten the screws on Steve's life. When Amy was only eight months old, we were elated when I learned I was pregnant with our third baby. Then we learned the grant money that paid Steve's salary would run out the month the baby was due. He panicked. By some miracle, God kept me calm.

As the baby grew and kicked inside me, both fear and faith wrestled inside Steve. He grappled with God on his own, silently asking Him to reveal Himself each day. He studied Scripture when he was alone, and even, without my knowledge, ordered copies of original documents from Israel. After sending out résumés to every educational research and development center in the area, then east of the Mississippi, we learned there were no openings anywhere. By October, I began asking God if He realized how close this was coming to our baby's due date.

Around that time, a new members' class was starting at church. I badly wanted to go, but worried how Steve would react. Finally, I just asked him if he minded me joining the church without him.

"Go ahead," he said. "But I don't want to." It was still a letdown.

Finally, the last week in October, Steve was invited to interview at Research for Better Schools, an educational research center in Philadelphia. It was our only nibble for a new job. Only two hours away, it seemed a perfect place for us. Our closest relatives, Steve's sister Cindy and her husband, Bob, lived there with their son. What could be more perfect? Early on Halloween day, Steve kissed the girls and me good-bye and took the train to Philly for his interview. Shortly after he left, our pastor, Jan Senneker, called asking if he might stop by later that evening to talk to me about membership.

"That would be great," I said, later wondering how this would sit with Steve.

Around two the afternoon, Steve called, obviously happy. "They offered me the job! I accepted. That's okay with you, isn't it?"

"It sure is! Congratulations! Say, Pastor Senneker wants to visit us tonight."

His tone changed completely. "What's he coming for?"

I explained about the membership class. Steve was less than excited, but agreed he could come. The job news called for a celebration, and on the way home, he stopped at the market and loaded up two large bags with ginger ale, mixed nuts, popcorn, chocolates, and more Halloween candy.

The pastor finally arrived around 9:00 p.m., after the last trick-or-treater left. While I went into the kitchen to fix a tray of party food, Steve began asking questions about his lingering doubts on the Bible and the Christian life. I brought in sodas and mixed nuts, but soon realized the two were deep in conversation and ducked back into the kitchen.

It seemed like their talk took forever. For almost an hour their voices, low and confidential, floated back to me. I stood out of view in the same corner where I had often prayed for grace and forgiveness. Then there was silence. I peeked into the living room to see Steve sitting in the black rocking chair with his head quietly bowed. He looked up and said, "I accept."

Thankfully, Pastor Senneker called to me. "Virelle, please join us. We have wonderful news! Tell her, Steve."

In the same soft voice he used months earlier to tell me I had become an unloving wife, he now said, "I've invited Christ into my life."

For one split second I doubted he really meant it. But both men were smiling and had tears in their eyes. And I knew. I just knew.

God kept me from leaping up and down. Instead, I smiled back at Steve, my head spinning. Pastor Senneker beamed and put his arms around us both and prayed. Then he offered advice about praying together daily; making Christ the center of our life; committing our marriage and family, our new job, and our home, all to Him from this day onward. Then he hugged us both and left.

I hardly knew what to do. My heart was quiet, and my mouth finally silent. I gave Steve another big hug and thanked God over and over in my heart. Steve shared that on the train that day, he knew he was going to be converted that night. God was unrelenting in His pursuit. Steve thought, *Why fight it any longer?*

Since that night, we've always remembered Halloween as Steve's spiritual birthday, the night he was born into the family of God. What a miracle! But there were more miracles to come, in fact, sooner than we even wanted.

CHAPTER 5

God's Surprises

Steve phoned me at noon the next day from work. "Guess what? Research for Better Schools just called. The funding needed to pay my salary fell through."

"It did? Just like that?" I felt a moment of panic. *What if Steve dumps his new faith over this?*

Instead of sounding grim, he was lighthearted. "God must have a better idea, don't you think?"

"Oh, yes." I tried to sound hopeful. "I'm sure He does," I added, looking down at my watermelon-shaped belly. With only six weeks to my due date, God would have to work fast. Babies don't wait. *You're hearing all this, aren't You, Lord?*

Later that day, Steve called again. "I never told you, but this place in Cambridge, Massachusetts, called me last week for an interview, but I told them you probably wouldn't move this late in your pregnancy. Dr. Coleman said I should go if they called me again. They just did. What do you think?" Dr. Coleman was Steve's boss.

"What kind of place is it?"

"It's a big research facility near Harvard, very avante garde. They want me to fly up tomorrow. I think I should check it out. Is that okay with you?"

I hesitated. Moving that far away seemed risky, especially now. We didn't know anyone there. Still, there wasn't much choice. This was our only opening. "I guess you'd better go. I'll ask our friends to pray."

At dawn Steve was on a plane, and drinking coffee in Cambridge by ten o'clock. After he went through a round of interviews, he was told the job was his if he wanted it, at a salary nearly twice what he was making at Johns Hopkins. They wanted him to start in three weeks, right after Thanksgiving. My mind was reeling.

"This must be our answer to prayer!" Steve filled me in excitedly from an office phone. "I think I should say yes, don't you?"

"I guess so, but be there in three weeks? I'm due in six weeks. Where are we going to live? How can we do that? Not many apartments will take three kids and a dog." My heart began to pound just thinking about it. Lauren had just settled into first grade. *Lord, are You hearing this?*

"We'll have to trust God, won't we? It'll be our first adventure together as Christians." What could I say to that? This was a new Steve for sure.

"Okay. I'm in." Why argue? It was a done deal. We'd move to Massachusetts. I couldn't even spell it yet.

Steve came home that night and broke the news to Lauren. She was thrilled at the prospect of a new school and a neighborhood full of friends. Her school had been anything but exciting in Baltimore because most of her friends had moved out to the suburbs earlier that summer. Lauren was lonely. She even had an imaginary playmate. This would be a welcome change for her. Now to tell Pastor Senneker and

our friends at Bible study about the move, and of course, our family. I
dialed the phone thinking, *No one's going to believe this!*

Things happened fast. Really fast. Steve's new company took care
of everything. Friends kept Amy overnight while the company flew the
three of us a few days later to Massachusetts to meet a realtor from
Lexington, a gorgeous historic community twenty minutes west of
Cambridge. We hadn't a penny in savings, but my mother had loaned
us a thousand dollars the night before, just in case we needed it.

I was right. No landlord in his right mind would take three kids
and a dog, but the realtor, who "happened" to be a Christian, showed
us a brand-new house in Lexington on a quiet street near the edge of
town. The builder needed to sell it and was ready to deal. Where would
we get the down payment? Our realtor told us his parents made small
loans for people he recommended. They loaned us the rest of the down
payment. We signed the deal and within two hours managed to apply
for a mortgage, choose eight rooms of wallpaper, and show Lauren her
new school. The next morning we were back home, dizzy with excitement.

Leaving Baltimore was wrenching. Our Bible study buddies sent us
off with an evening of prayer, great food, whoops of joy, a new *Living
Bible*, and promises to come and visit. We all cried. I couldn't imagine
life without them. We had no one in the Boston area, no church, no
family or friends, not even a doctor to deliver our baby. Had we both
not been so certain God was moving us, it would have been frightening. Instead, we shared the tingle of adventure.

Movers soon packed our rented row house into stacks of neatly la-
beled boxes. I had nothing to do but visit friends and make phone calls.
It was a first-class company. Steve's new employer paid for every detail
of our move, every phone call, plane flight, and meal until we arrived—
even gas for the car. Our favorite neighbors, the Gilberts, invited us

for Thanksgiving dinner. The next morning we piled both kids and the dog into our car, waved a tearful good-bye, and headed north to our new home.

No plan is without kinks. Two days later, on a snowy New England day, a gracious hotel welcomed us all, even our dog. Next door sprawled the gargantuan Burlington Mall, and ten minutes away our new home was getting its last touches of paper and paint. Lauren was delirious with excitement, jumping up and down over her first real snow. Every hour she asked, "Can we go outside and make a snowman now, Daddy?"

There we sat in the hotel, waiting for our furniture to arrive.

It might have been fun, but on the second day, we descended into misery when Amy began cutting her first molars. Our champion screamer, now unable to sleep, made it all but impossible to leave the hotel room. After one fiasco ruining everyone's meal in the hotel dining room, we ate in shifts or ordered room service. Nothing helped her, not even baby aspirin and topical painkillers at near-dangerous levels. The simpler choice was to take turns babysitting Amy, walking the dog, putting Oragel on her gums, keeping Lauren busy, traipsing around the mall, walking the dog one more time, ordering room service, and trying not to come unglued. With our closing only two days away, Steve began feverishly calling the movers.

Our worst fears were confirmed: our furniture was indeed lost. Maybe it went to New Jersey. No one could say for sure, but they promised to find it. Soon. When it was time for the closing, our realtor, a bachelor in his forties, babysat both our five-year-old in overdrive and our fussy toddler in the attorney's waiting room while we signed papers to buy our miracle house. I should have been ecstatic, but on the way back to the hotel, I turned to Steve and said, "If I go back there, I'll lose my mind. If you'll watch Amy, I'll take Lauren and walk around the mall again."

"No problem."

Halfway around the Burlington Mall, I began to feel ill. "Honey, Mommy's got to sit down." We found a bench. I tried to get comfortable, but pain began moving up my back, while terrible cramps gripped my abdomen. *This can't be labor yet. I must have eaten something that made me sick.* If only I could call Steve. But I had the car! He couldn't even get to me. Panicky, I prayed, *Oh, God, help me! I don't know what to do!*

"Mommy, we can sit here. You'll feel better." Lauren patted my arm, her blue eyes showing grown-up concern. "I'll ask Jesus to help us." She folded her hands, bowed her head, and prayed silently with tremendous earnestness. I remembered the day I told Lauren God was giving us another baby sister or brother. She dashed into the dining room, folded her hands and prayed. "Mommy," she announced moments later. "We're having a brother."

"Oh, honey. We don't know what this baby will be. God will give us whatever is best."

"Yes, but it's a brother. I asked Him, and He said yes." I worried for months how she would feel if God let her down.

As the two of us sat together on a cement bench with flowers and trees surrounding us, I wondered if we'd find out sooner than we planned. Lauren continued patting my arm, while I tried to sit still and muster up faith. In a little while, my back pain subsided and the cramps as well. I stood up to see if I could walk, and I could. "Come on, honey. Let's go find Daddy and Amy." We made our way slowly to the car.

Back at the hotel, Steve and Amy were a welcome sight, and room service food never tasted better. Steve had received a call that our furniture had been found and, yes, it was in New Jersey. It would be delivered tomorrow to 36 Webb Street. Hallelujah! Enough adventure. We needed a place to call home.

And a beautiful one it was, a garrison colonial, cadet blue cedar with brick on the bottom, twenty-six sunny windows, and black shutters all around. It even had a fireplace. When the van finally backed up our driveway, laying a ramp up the front steps, Steve and I watched in amazement as they carried our furniture inside.

We had little in those days, just our blue couch and the black rocker, a table and four kitchen chairs, a few lamps and our beds and dressers. My mother had given us an antique desk and my father's wall clock and some artwork. The girls scrambled up the stairs, squealing with happiness at their new room, the baby's room and bathroom down the hallway, and our huge bedroom the size of the living room below. With only our bed and antique dresser, it looked like a gymnasium. But it was home, and more beautiful than we'd ever imagined.

"Hey, everyone!" Steve called from the kitchen door. "Look out back. We have visitors!"

Lauren bolted down the stairs with Amy tumbling behind. Both girls joined us excitedly in the kitchen. "Who's here, Daddy?"

"Come and see!" Steve hoisted Amy high to see out the window while Lauren and I peeked out the back door. Yup! We had visitors, all right. Eight of them: a mama and papa pheasant and six little babies who lived in the conservation land behind our house. A welcoming committee!

"Oh, Daddy, can we feed them? Please?" Lauren jumped up and down.

"All we have are crackers. How about that?" I said.

Pheasants, it seems, love crackers. They ate like piranha and waited for more. We wondered how they'd survived before we moved in. Our feathered family adopted us—they showed off their babies and screeched at our back door every morning before sunrise, confident breakfast was on the way.

Soon it would be Christmas and my mother would arrive to help with the new baby. The girls would make friends and play in the snow for the first time. 36 Webb Street became a home of many miracles, and even more surprises.

God set us on an accelerated course becoming a Christian family. He must have known it wouldn't be easy. He wasted no time getting started.

CHAPTER 6

Fork in the Road

I was over-the-moon happy in Lexington. Lauren had a gang of new girlfriends whisking her off to ice skate or play dolls or have lunch. Amy missed her constant presence, but followed me around the house dragging her moo cow on wheels, soon named her "security cow." I unpacked boxes, settling dressers and closets, aiming for a small sense of order before our new arrival came. Things fell into place a little at a time and our new house began to feel like home.

My mother arrived a week before Christmas to help out. She read stories to the girls and kept us fed while Steve and I put up a skinny Christmas tree, the last one on the lot. We strung it with lights, popcorn, and whatever ornaments were buried in the basement. It provided a tinkling backdrop of falling needles all through the holiday. Late one night, Steve and I quickly pulled together a few presents for Lauren and Amy. Mother bought us New England–style ball fringe curtains for all the windows. With her help, we managed to hang them and put a few pictures on the walls. Things were coming together nicely until one morning just before Christmas, when the unthinkable happened.

As if I needed a reason to stop running up and down stairs on a mission to find Lauren dry socks, I slipped at the top and the rest is history. Mother, Lauren, and Amy and a few playmates watched helplessly as I fell down all thirteen slick hardwood stairs, hitting my head and back on each one. Lauren burst out laughing, watching such a ludicrous event. I tried to laugh it off, too, but couldn't. I headed for the couch, while Mother franticly paged Steve at work with an emergency at home. Thinking I'd gone into labor, he arrived twenty minutes later looking ghastly. By that time I was comfortable and sipping tea on the couch. I suffered a mild concussion and bruises up and down my back like the rungs of a ladder. Amazingly, the doctor said the baby would be fine. It added a little more excitement to Christmas. Since that day, I walk down stairs gripping the railing like an old lady.

Christmas Eve brought snow floating down in big, fat flakes. Steve, Lauren, and I crunched our way to the car for the candlelight service at Grace Chapel. Mother stayed home to watch a television special with Amy and tuck her in early.

Lexington, wreathed and lighted, was magical in the falling snow. Lauren squealed with delight. Grace Chapel's sanctuary was packed. When the usher took one look at my very pregnant form, we were escorted to the second row, where everyone smiled and squeezed in to make room. Steve was given a folding chair in the aisle next to me. The sound of the magnificent organ filled the sanctuary with triumphant carols, as hundreds of voices joined in worship. I was filled with joy and gratefulness.

Only two months earlier we were still praying for a job, and Steve wasn't even a believer. Now, I could hardly take in all God had given us. The gift of His Son's death on the cross had transformed our lives dramatically. Now we were a Christian family. A real one. And God wasn't done with us yet. A new baby danced inside me to the worshipful music. *Oh, Father, help me learn how to love You back. Thank You for our new home, for Steve's new faith, for this church, for our new baby, for our new life here.* Nothing could get better than this.

But it did. Just three days later our first son, David Steven, was born by caesarian section. He was perfect, blond and sweet. Steve cried. I was stunned. We were so certain it would be a girl named "Sarah." But Lauren wasn't surprised at all. "I told you, Mommy. I asked God for a brother and He said yes."

"Yes, He did, honey. Yes, He did."

Reality soon set in. We discovered three kids are a lot more work than two. Probably double, at least. Just keeping up with laundry and meals, changing two babies, reading stories, doing minimal housework, and we were buried. *How does anybody do this?* I wondered. On top of it, we were clearly reaping the results of several years of disagreement over discipline. Our five-year-old now proved herself a master at working one parent against the other. We needed help. Fast!

Fortunately, Gail and Gordon MacDonald picked up on our need. Having begun their pastorate at Grace Chapel only three months earlier, they took a personal interest in us, mentoring us invisibly with honesty, friendship, and example. Gordon regularly drove into Cambridge for lunch with Steve, and Gail occasionally stopped by to drop off books on parenting and spiritual growth she thought I'd enjoy. We grew to love them both and watched like hawks to see how real Christian families behaved.

Gradually, both Steve and I recognized our need to "grow up" as parents and work together. Since I'd played the heavy so long, I needed to back off and let Steve handle more discipline, even if I thought he was too soft. That was hard, but over time, he emerged as a strong but gentle father whose words carried a lot of weight with our children. When he lowered the boom and grounded Lauren or gave her a spanking, it was both rare and fair. That left me able to enjoy her more with a lot less tension.

Within a year or so, Steve and I had agreed on a few unbendable goals for our children: honesty, obedience, and kindness. We communicated with each other before making decisions. Now Lauren couldn't drag out her favorite ploy, "Daddy said it was okay," but she certainly tried.

God gave me a new calmness, and a firm resolve. "Sorry, honey. Daddy and I already talked with you about that already. It's not okay."

"Well, yesterday Daddy said . . ."

"Shall we talk to him together again?"

"No, I guess not." Disgruntled, she soon gave up, but only temporarily.

Learning to work together as parents was an ongoing challenge. It was easy to get caught off guard, leading us often to Gordon and Gail and others for advice. We found that most parents struggle with their role, especially Christians. God gave us mentors to show us how. Parenting is a difficult and humbling role, teaching us often that only God is adequate for the job.

Our neighbors began a custom of dropping in often for coffee, enjoying Amy and our new baby, David. They invited Lauren to play with their children, even taxiing her to and from school and ice skating lessons. Figure skating became her passion. She would dress Amy up in tan tights and skating outfits and pretend they were ice dancing on the hardwood floors. As soon as David could crawl and stand up, he was dressed up, too, and paraded into our bedroom in the mornings for another elaborate show. He learned early to smile on cue.

Feeling the inner nudge from God to reach out to neighborhood kids, I began a Good News Club, much like Mrs. Foley's club in Baltimore. A teenager in the area babysat Amy and David one afternoon a week while a dozen or more kids from ages four to twelve poured into our living room for Bible stories, snacks, and "gold nugget" rewards for attendance and learning verses. Soon, Amy preferred to squeeze in between the bigger kids on the couch and listen, too. While many of those children came to know Christ as Savior, I grew and learned along with them. Many of the Bible lessons were new to me, too.

But into this happy picture conflict was brewing, in fact several conflicts. The first involved my mother. We had issues. When Mother left after David was born, I breathed a heavy sigh of relief as usual. Angry words were not our problem, but a long history of unresolved hurts and disappointment in each other were. Irritation colored every interaction, even phone calls.

Mother and I were opposites. She saw nothing wrong in living by a litany of half-truths that suited her at the time. "Tell her I'm not home;" "Don't tell anyone about this;" and her favorite warning, "Only a foul bird betrays its own nest." Secrecy was the family code. Even as a young child, it bothered me.

Now that I had thrown myself whole hog into the Christian camp, I served a God whose name was Truth. Mother thought of me as an embarrassment and a fanatic. She questioned me at length about my choices and voiced her negative opinions freely. Frankly, living as far away as possible from my mother was fine with me. Lexington was only one hundred and fifty miles away, but it would do.

But Mother loved her grandchildren dearly. She was stellar in that role and regularly came for weekend visits and every holiday. I could be pleasant for a few days at a time, but the strain of her visits left me cranky and exhausted. We all waved good-bye after one such visit as she drove away in her white Chevy, tooting the horn all the way down the street. Alone at last in my kitchen, I cried out to God, "Lord, I don't love my mother! Is that really so bad?"

That's your choice, came His gentle reply to my heart, *but you and I can't go much farther like that.*

Rats.

"Lord, I'm *willing* to love her, but You'll have to give it to me. I just don't have it." He'd certainly given me renewed love for Steve, better than before. Maybe it would work with Mother, too. I'm glad I didn't know how God would answer that prayer.

Problems began brewing over Steve's job. His company expected him to work weekends and even holidays in addition to traveling quite often. We seldom saw him. Every Friday night the kids colored pictures for a "Welcome Home, Daddy!" party, and every Sunday or Monday meant seeing that his clothes were freshly ironed and packed for another business trip. Managing our home, Lauren's school projects, sick kids, and babies waking at night fell to me. Loneliness and a grumbling attitude weren't far behind. Tensions crept back into our marriage.

One morning I sat on the couch and tried to read my Bible while Amy entertained David in the playroom. Nothing made sense. Feeling my heart torn with resentment, I prayed. *Lord, what's wrong with me? I can't snap out of this miserable attitude. I don't like being alone all the time when Steve's away. It isn't fair to the kids or me! Won't You do something to change things?*

Learn to love him in a new way, came His reply, *without complaining or expecting anything in return.* This didn't sound too fair, either.

But how, Lord? Isn't that asking a lot of me right now? Granted, Steve's job was far more stressful than we'd expected. Even though it seemed glamorous to stay in five-star hotels with telephones in the bathrooms, he missed us a lot and hated being away so much. My complaining certainly made it worse. I had no idea how to change.

Then God whispered again. *Release him to Me. Trust Me to take care of your needs.* I prayed just that. It was easier than I thought and relief was immediate. Now all I had to do was learn this new way of loving him, without complaining or expecting anything. No doubt about it. That would be hard.

I started small. Maybe a love note tucked in his suitcase would help. The kids made drawings and put small stuffed animals inside, too. Steve felt loved and missed the moment he unpacked. We had fun thinking up small surprises for Daddy. The bigger surprise came as God changed my complaining attitude, melting it into renewed love and support. Friday night "Welcome Home, Daddy!" parties were also less stressed once Steve began bringing home one of Lexington's famous Greek pizzas.

Gradually, I discovered glimmers of happiness from someplace deeper in my core, knowing I was obeying God in tiny ways no one else saw. I felt His pleasure, His smile. It warmed me down to my toes. Our marriage grew stronger in weeks, not months. We were a team now, a threefold team: God, Steve, and me. Just in the nick of time, too. Freight train–sized changes were heading our way, changes I would hate right from the start.

Is It My Turn Yet?

J ust when things seemed to be going well again, Steve's job began heating up miserably, often requiring him to work late into the night. He was chronically exhausted. Being a determined, goal-oriented person, he was also trying to read three or four chapters a night in his Bible before bedtime. After working late one night, he came home and ate a sandwich with me in the living room.

"I can't stay awake any longer, honey." I kissed him good night and headed to bed.

"I'll just read a little and be up in a minute." Opening to Psalm 127, he read verses 1 and 2: "Unless the Lord builds the house, its builders labor in vain. Unless the Lord watches over the city, the watchmen stand guard in vain. In vain you rise early and stay up late, toiling for food to eat—for he grants sleep to those he loves." *That's incredible! That's just what I'm doing!* he thought. With that, he closed his Bible and went to bed.

The next morning, Steve told me about the verses. We both read

the rest of the psalm: "Sons are a heritage from the Lord, children a reward from him. Like arrows in the hands of a warrior are sons born in
one's youth. Blessed is the man whose quiver is full of them. They will
not be put to shame when they contend with their enemies in the gate"
(vv. 3–5). Children matter a lot to God. Our family mattered a lot. We
both knew our time as a family had dwindled badly.

Not long afterward, Steve was again working late at his desk, when
he tipped his chair back and looked around at the many people still in
his office. *Why,* he wondered, *didn't I see this before? Almost everyone
who works here is either single or divorced. That's a bad sign.* This avante
garde company provided not only a French chef who cooked three out-
standing meals a day, and a basketball court, but also a childcare center with extra hours at both ends of the day. No wonder everyone
arrived early and worked late. This office was their home. Some even
had refrigerators and cots in their room!

Steve left heavyhearted and prayed all the way home. When he
came in the door after the kids were in bed, I could see that something
in his expression had changed. His jaw was locked in resolve. "We need
to talk," he began. We sat together in front of a crackling fire in the
fireplace while he related his observations. "This job is killing our family," he said. I knew he was right. Steve's work often bullied our limited
family time into a small corner of life. Trying to explore options yielded
few ideas. I couldn't argue when he said, "The truth is, if we don't make
a change, our family won't survive either."

The silence was pregnant with possibilities, most of them bad.
"What do we do now?"

"Pray for a new job. I'll start sending out résumés this week. There
are lots of research centers in the Boston area. I'm sure I can find another job that's as good as this one."

Of course he could. I was certain of it.

But he couldn't. Since most research centers function on "soft money," meaning money received from public or private grants, and funding in education was seriously down that year, no one was hiring. In fact, education professionals were being laid off. In short, there were no jobs in Boston.

"We won't have to move, will we, Steve?" I couldn't bear the thought. Our new life was perfect here. We loved our new church, the friendly neighborhood, especially Lauren's elementary school. Leave all this? God wouldn't ask us to do that after bringing us here on a path of miracles. I was sure of it, adding with a smile, "Let's pray harder. I'm sure there's something good out there for you!"

Weeks went by with no nibbles. Then months. We invited Christian friends over, hoping they'd pray for us, or offer Steve a job, or at least commiserate. Nothing happened. Nothing except one phone call on a cold March day.

Steve phoned from work. "I got a call from the New York State Education Department in Albany. They want me to interview for a job in educational research. It's a budgeted item; no more working on contracts."

"Did you send them a résumé?"

"No. Someone else must have suggested my name. I think I should go, don't you?"

"Go? Why would you do that?" Albany sounded like the other side of a desert. We'd lived there far too long in college and graduate school. Beside that, my mother lived there. No, Albany was out of the question. Mississippi maybe, but not Albany.

"Honey, I need another job. I just found out our company won't have the money to pay my salary soon. I should at least interview. They want me to fly over tomorrow morning."

"Oh, great! Steve, promise me you won't take a job in Albany."

"I'll check it out. We prayed, remember?"

Maybe so, but this wasn't the answer I wanted. God knew that. He wouldn't ask us to make this drastic, horrible change.

At six the next morning, Steve drove in the dark to Logan Airport for an early flight, a puddle hop from Boston to Albany. By noon, I'd given Amy and David an early lunch and tucked them in for a nap when the phone rang. It was Steve already. He had a lot to say. "They've offered me the job. It's a small salary cut, but this will be better for our family. I'll still have to travel, but not all the time. I can be home most nights and always on the weekends."

"Are you serious? They offered it to you just like that?"

"Yes they did, and I'd like to take it," he said quietly, adding after a long pause, "Will you come?"

Would I come? Did I have a choice? I knew exactly whom to blame, and it wasn't Steve. "Are you sure? I mean really sure?" *Lord, don't You have another idea out there?*

"I really think it's the right decision."

I knew Steve didn't like this any more than I did. He was doing his best for us.

"Okay, I'll come. How soon?"

"They want me to start Monday. I'll have to put my notice in tomorrow and work both jobs for a few weeks. I'm going to check out real estate next."

"Isn't this happening a little fast?" *Lord, we need to talk. This plan of Yours stinks!* "I need a little time to deal with this."

"Thanks, honey. I love you and I'll talk to you later."

I fell to my knees and sobbed. This was exactly the opposite of what I wanted. *Lord, how could You do this to me, to our whole family? We're so happy here. Don't you care?* Suddenly, a new reality hit. I'd have to live near my mother. *Oh, God, this is too much! I can't do it!*

All through the kids' naptime, I cried and prayed. Finally, limp with spent emotion, I gave up. The fight was over. I'd do what God, and Steve, wanted. But I wouldn't like it. I overheard myself committing our whole life in Lexington to Him, especially the children in our Good News Club, the precious neighbors and friends who already felt like family, our church home and those we loved so much at Grace Chapel. It felt like a great unraveling of my will, yet again. *Could there be anything more in life this hard?* I wondered. (Even the question shames me now.)

Yes, there could. At four o'clock the phone rang. It was Steve again. He was standing in my mother's kitchen. She was delirious with the news. Next to them stood an equally happy realtor who was about to sell Steve a new house.

"Honey, I found us a house," he began slowly. "I think you'll like it. It's new. It's in Guilderland, in the best school district in the area."

"What color is it?"

"It's green. It's small but it has four bedrooms and a beautiful lot. It's on the edge of a big woods the kids will love. Is it okay with you if I buy it?"

"Sure. Buy it." What good would it do quibbling over a house now? We were already losing everything I loved. I figured five years from now we'd build another house. It was only fair.

But we didn't. We ended up living there thirty-one years. Our kids loved the woods and trees, the school, and we all loved our neighbors. God obviously placed our family in the home He chose. Many of our new neighbors and their children came to know Christ as Savior and Lord. I papered and painted every room, like my mother had years ago when we moved to the town of Mexico. Steve eventually replaced the kitchen we so disliked with a new one, added a huge family room, and planted raspberry bushes one year on Mother's Day. It was home, and most of the time, a happy one.

I'm ashamed to say that making peace with our small green house took me years of dealing with discontent and envy. I dreamed of a bigger house with a nicer kitchen, a real dining room, larger bedrooms, another bathroom, bigger closets, and a two-car garage. Steve urged me to find one. I tried every year, but nothing felt as warm and welcoming as our home.

I finally gave up my vague dreams of happiness in a bigger house. A smaller surrender than I'd imagined, one day I prayed, "Okay, God, You choose for me." How simple. Although I still wrestled with it seasonally, I finally let it go and made the place of my "confinement" beautiful, the way a comfortable pair of slippers is beautiful. And it was for a long, long time.[1]

Living near my mother proved a strange answer to my kitchen confession a year or so earlier. Had I known God would move us to a house ten miles away from hers, I might not have prayed so honestly. But I did, and He did. The results were more than surprising.

In the weeks prior to our move to Albany, I lined up prayer warriors, knowing hard times were ahead living so close to my mother. Jewel Hubley, whose husband, Nate, taught Steve's new believers' class at Grace Chapel, offered this wise advice: "Virelle, I'll tell you what I've found true. There are many solutions to a problem, but anything next to love is only second best." Zinger! Love again. I already knew I couldn't manufacture it. God would have to give it big time.

And He did. My mother and I moved into a new stage of reality—adulthood. I knew there were times when I'd shown anger, said things I regretted, and held grudges against her for years. One day I invited her over and confessed them all, asking her forgiveness. She claimed she couldn't remember any of it (now I know that's almost possible), but agreed to forgive me if it would make me happy.

It didn't work well in reverse. I tried to press her to acknowledge her own mistakes, but without success. Mother seldom, if ever, admitted fallibility. That was hard. Since then, I'm learning forgiveness brings its own relief. Even when others don't recognize or acknowledge their offenses, simply forgiving them is enough.

In the twenty or so years before Mother's Alzheimer's set in, we filled in the gaps of lost family life with lots of hoopla over birthdays and Christmas, decorating the tree, sharing meals at her home and ours. The kids loved my mother. She was truly a fantastic grandmother. Our communication never achieved the deeper levels of faith or intimacy I craved, but the inner tension gradually abated. For intimacy, we substituted shared lives, kids' soccer games and concerts, photo shoots for proms and graduations.

I'm grateful now for those good memories, more than I ever imagined. God gave the love I needed, when I asked, right when I needed it. Good thing. My need for His strong love didn't diminish. In fact, He stretched me until I thought I'd rip in two, just to make room for more. I would need it all.

Note

1. Portions of this chapter have been retold in *Donkeys Still Talk: Hearing God's Voice When You're Not Listening* (Colorado Springs: Navpress, 2004), 42–47.

CHAPTER 8

Growing a Life

Maybe we thought God required it. I'm not sure, but each time we moved to another home, Steve and I gave it back to Him to do as He pleased. It dawned on me while struggling with yet another set of clean sheets one Friday afternoon, that He'd taken that literally. In the first six months alone in Lexington, we'd entertained enough houseguests to qualify as a B & B. One weekend after another friends, relatives, old neighbors, even complete strangers showed up. I cranked out nice suppers and breakfasts, and tried to make the house look presentable, but by the time folks left on Sunday afternoon, I was exhausted. We both loved having company, but after a while it got old.

I sat down on the green studio couch in the playroom (our first "guest room") to grumble at God. *What's up here, Lord? I feel like a servant in my own home.* A pregnant silence followed. I sat and thought about that. Hm-m-m. Maybe that's the idea. *Are You trying to teach me to be a servant? Lord, do I really have to learn all that now? Couldn't we just enjoy our home alone sometimes?*

Not just yet. The parade continued longer than we expected. Our guests added way more than dirty laundry. They injected loads of spice and fun into our family life and piled up memories we'd never have had without them. Because the churches we attended actively supported foreign missions, our kids learned early to wrap their arms around people from China, Nepal, Vietnam, France, Germany, Russia, Guatemala, and India. American regulars included a few singles and their kids, one lonely fireman, elderly drop-ins on Christmas Eve, a young woman with mental illness, several lonely college students, a teenage foreign student from Guatemala who became like a daughter, even a couple of sailors and their wives who visited one Thanksgiving with nowhere to go. The best part? Many became lifetime friends who fine-tuned our sensitivity to the wide variety of flowers in God's garden.

It was fun, but still work. As our kids grew older, everyone pitched in cleaning the house, carrying in groceries, and changing linens. Entertaining wasn't always constant, but became a family project. I learned to appreciate my mother's gift for instant hospitality. She never expressed it this way, but made a habit of treating family like company and company like family. The formula worked. People always felt at home. When they offered to help, I found them a job chopping a salad, setting the table, or reading to the kids. Some stayed way past dinner and actually moved in for a few days, even a few months.

Our longest learning curve in hospitality came late one afternoon in June as three Vietnamese refugees tumbled out of a van carrying little more than paper bags holding the remnants of a lifetime. A member of our neighborhood Bible study had asked for prayer for thirty-three family members who remained in Vietnam during the fall of her homeland to the communists. We agreed to help, learning quickly that most had barely escaped with their lives, especially our guests Mr. and Mrs. Huong and their four-year-old grandson, Gung.

"Good morning!" the small gray-haired man said, and he almost saluted. Standing directly behind him was his gaunt little wife in a long Vietnamese dress, her dark but graying hair pulled tightly into a bun. She smiled with her face pointed toward the ground. I realized she had no teeth. Neither did Gung, or at least very few.

Steve held out his hand to welcome them. I did the same and tried to put an arm around Mrs. Huong and Gung, but they pulled back shyly. "Welcome to our home!" I smiled broadly. "This is your home now, too." Our three eager kids were smiling right behind me, anxious to meet their new playmate. "Oh, this is Lauren, she's seven; and Amy who's almost four; and David, who's two."

"Good morning!" Mr. Huong smiled and nodded again, ruffling David's blond head. Mrs. Huong hung behind, holding Gung's hand. Steve cast me a knowing look. He realized we'd just heard all the English they knew. Life at our house would be interesting indeed.

Very.

Gung, whose daddy was one of the Huong's nine adult children, ran over to a tricycle on the driveway. Squealing with delight, he leaped on top and started peddling fast. Just as quickly, Mrs. Huong smacked him on the side of the head and yanked him off, wheeling it over to Amy and Dave with mumbled apologies.

"He can ride it!" they both said, wheeling it back.

She shook her head firmly. The answer was no. We would quickly learn Vietnamese grandparents play an active, even powerful, role in their children and grandchildren's lives. Once children are past the little and cute stage, discipline is swift and unmistakable. Even harsh in our view. Before that, as David soon enjoyed, children were indulged and spoiled royally. Especially blond blue-eyed little boys.

In his homeland, Mr. Huong once held a major place in the government and was accustomed to being chauffeured in limos, giving orders, and running his office and family with an iron hand. He probably had bodyguards and a staff of servants. Now, homeless and in his sixties, all that was taken away, except his role in the family. Everyone obeyed him, including his seven adult children who were hosted by other area families. (Two other children were unable to escape.)

Language was our initial challenge. The Huongs both spoke flawless French. With Steve's fairly firm grip of the language and my smattering of college French, we managed. At night, we held English lessons in the living room, and we tried to learn some Vietnamese. It became a dance. French in the kitchen, English upstairs, Vietnamese in between the three Huongs. Our kids never knew what anyone was saying. One night as Steve and I tucked our children in for bed, we all burst out laughing, realizing we were speaking broken English!

There were more problems. David was being spoiled rotten. He'd push Gung away from his toys and demand his own way. When I corrected him, Mr. and Mrs. Huong would pick him up and carry my son, their little blond emperor, away. I had to stop David's behavior, and I did, but no one was happy with me for a while.

One day, Flora Lam, a close Chinese friend, arrived to join me for a ladies' retreat in New Hampshire. My bags were packed and in the front hall when the doorbell rang. Mr. Huong answered it as Flora entered carrying two large bags of clothing and canned food for them. When she set them down on the hall floor, Mr. Huong pointed at the bags, then at me, and motioned for me to carry them downstairs. I did it automatically, and then thought, *Wait a minute! He thinks he's in charge of me, too!*

I'd never been ordered around like a servant before.

Flora chuckled about it on the way out the door, but suggested

Steve and I had to have a talk with Mr. Huong. Soon.

I was elected. On Monday morning after the retreat, I spoke to Mr. Huong in a mixture of limited French, English, and hand signals. Keeping it simple, I said, "Mr. Huong, when Steve is at home, he is in charge." I was glad Steve wasn't hearing this.

He nodded enthusiastically.

"But when Steve is at work, I am in charge."

He looked at me questioningly. I repeated it more slowly in French this time, looking up "in charge" in my French/English dictionary. "Je suis la chargé d'affaires ici." Overstatement, perhaps, but he got the message, his expression changing to one of extreme disappointment. He turned and went quietly downstairs. I heard voices behind their bedroom door.

The kitchen was a different matter. I had to give up ground.

While I made dinner, Mr. Huong often hovered near the stove and watched me cook. He'd motion to his wife to come quickly and take over, or at least help me. With a little bow, she'd oblige by adding more oil to whatever it was and cranking the burners up high. Smoke and spattering oil sent Steve flying to get the windows and doors open. Clearly, Mr. Huong was still in charge here, barking orders in Vietnamese to his wife, sniffing through my cabinets for the right spices. It must have never tasted quite right.

One day, while driving home, we passed them walking in a line back from the local market about a mile away. Mr. Huong strode confidently down the middle of the street with Mrs. Huong following directly behind him carrying a paper bag on top of her head. Gung skipped along in the wake of her flapping dress. We offered them a ride, but they smiled and waved us on.

"How do you suppose they did that?" I wondered out loud. "They don't speak more than ten English words yet."

"Beats me. We'll find out soon."

A few minutes later, the Huongs arrived home. With much fan-fare, they motioned us all out of the kitchen. Things crackled and smoked for about two hours. Wildly unfamiliar aromas filled the house.

"What are we eating tonight, Mommy?" Lauren said, her blue eyes wide with alarm.

"I have no idea, honey. Just taste it and be polite. Mrs. Huong is working hard in there." Frankly, several times I feared she'd burn the house down, but it never happened.

Call it our initiation to real Vietnamese food. The main course was ginger beef, or *bo-khō*, something like pot roast with spicy red gravy seasoned with fresh ginger, curry, anise, onion, garlic, and tomato paste served over white rice with carrots on the side. Sensational! It became Steve's favorite dish. Our kids asked for seconds. From that day on, we were hooked. (And I've included this recipe and another favorite at the end of this chapter for you to try.) I became Mrs. Huong's regular side-kick and student at the stove any time she wanted to cook.

Four months into this international experiment, someone offered the Huongs a free farmhouse complete with a flock of bantam reds in the country, where they often invited us for, you guessed it, chicken dinners. We missed them when they left, discovering over the years how much they had taught us, things like frugality, cheerfulness in spite of loss, and heightened honor and respect for older people.

I learned how hard being a servant really is. Too often my pushed-down pride shamed me when it rose in protest. Serving is humbling work and seldom noticed. Does it ever get easy? Not for me. I still chafe at times.

During these open-door years, I read many of Francis and Edith Schaeffer's books. Francis was usually over my head, but I found Edith's writing earthy, arty, honest, and true. In her book *L'Abri*, describing their life work in Switzerland ministering to the young and disillusioned in post-war Europe, she wrote about her struggles doing just what I was doing, caring for long-term, or at least frequent, houseguests. But she did it for years upon years, for huge housefuls at a time, often working in the kitchen until midnight so Francis could explore intellectual debates by the fire.

She had few, if any, mechanical "servants" like washers, dryers, and dishwashers. Fresh linens and sheets took far more work to launder and air dry. She grew vegetables and flowers in her garden to save money and provide quality food. She flung beauty around the house with flower arrangements, pinecones, candles, and greens. Francis led students to Christ over Edith's homemade pies and cakes, and she discipled them later in the kitchen as they washed dishes together at night.

I find that astounding! How did Edith do that? My guess is she learned it the hard way, like we all do. And she prayed, asking God to give her the mind of Christ.

That's the ticket! I began asking God for strength and cheerfulness, thanking Him daily for Edith's example. *Lord, I am selfishly born and remain to this day, one loving to be served. Change me, Lord. Remake me from the inside out into one who serves with a loving heart.*

I'd need that prayer more than I realized in the days to come.

Mrs. Huong's Bo-Khō (Ginger Beef)

1 lb flank steak	8–10 cloves minced garlic
4–5 tsp soy sauce	1 tbsp tomato paste
1 tsp curry powder	1 tsp salt
4 tbsp vegetable oil	2 C water or chicken broth
½ cup onion (more to taste)	2 small carrots
20 matchstick-thin slices ginger root	star anise (a few slices)

Cut meat into diagonal strips or squares. Season with curry powder and garlic. Sauté onions, anise, and ginger root in oil. Add meat, tomato paste, soy sauce, and brown. Add salt, water or broth, and cover. Cook 1 ½ to 2 hours. Add carrots the last half hour and cook until tender. (Optional: add 1 small can mushrooms and 1 lb snow peas.) Serve over hot cooked rice.

Vietnamese Fried Rice

Mix 1 egg and a little soy sauce. Fry in large fry pan in oil, turning over once. Put on chopping board and cut into thin strips. Sauté chopped meat and chopped onion. (Mrs. Huong used canned ham.) Add 1 or 2 tbsp tomato paste and fry in skillet a moment before adding meat. Stir thoroughly, and add 2 cups or more cooked white rice. Fry at high heat, stirring constantly. Add soy sauce to taste and sliced eggs. Adapt to taste, using pork, sausage, or small pieces of shrimp.

CHAPTER 9

God's Addition

In June, the same month our Vietnamese friends arrived, we received the stunning news that my husband's older cousin had taken her life at their home in Jamestown, New York, leaving five children ranging in age from fourteen to thirteen months. One week later, her husband followed suit.

A generous aunt and uncle, who lived in the same city, initially took in all the children. Adding these five to their own four kids soon proved to be too much. Because we lived 350 miles away in Albany, and had only once met the children, we just prayed . . . until one hot summer day around 5:30 p.m.

Steve walked in the front door from work and motioned for me to meet him on the stairs. Mrs. Huong was happily filling the kitchen with smoke. Clearly upset about something, he spoke in low tones. "The four older kids are okay, but no one can handle the baby."

"How do you know?"

"My mom told me today. They're considering putting him up for general adoption. She was crying."

I gasped. Put a family member up for adoption?

"Then, we'll take him!"

Tears filled Steve's eyes. "That's what I was hoping you'd say. Are you okay with that? It's already a little crazy around here."

"Of course! We always felt sad Dave would be the only boy. Now he'll have a little brother! Do you know anything about the baby?"

"Just that his name is Bob, same as my dad's. He's just over a year old and really cute."

"What a way to have a baby, huh? The kids will be excited. Can we tell them?"

"Not just yet. There's a lot of legal stuff involved. Let's see how it goes, then we'll tell them." We hugged on the stairs, both realizing something huge had just happened. That moment of perfect agreement felt, for us, like we'd conceived our new child.

We couldn't wait. At two and a half and almost four, David and Amy were a little small to understand, but Lauren, nearly eight, clasped her hands in breathless excitement. Two little brothers? God really over-answered her prayers!

Taking six months in court versus nine months in the womb, Bobby's adoption proved a lot more like giving birth than we'd imagined. It seems nothing happens quickly when lawyers are involved. Throughout the long waiting period, we gave the outcome to God many times. At last, a court date was set in Jamestown, just prior to Thanksgiving.

We drove the whole family out there and stayed with Steve's brother, Ron, and his wife, Candy. On the day of the hearing, Steve's grandmother and his aunt Marion invited Lauren, Amy, and David for the morning and lunch to their home on Barker Street in Jamestown, where Grandma had once moved when she was a bride of eighteen. Steve's dad, the oldest of six children, had been born in the upstairs bedroom. A lot of family history happened there.

"We won't be long," we assured her. "This is just a formality."

But it wasn't. The adoption hearing involved three lawyers: one for the baby, one for us, and one for a handful of other relatives who only recently decided to put their names in the hat, too. It lasted an entire day. Late in the afternoon, the judge asked Steve what it means for him to be a father. He faltered a moment, then broke down in tears and sobbed uncontrollably, something I'd never seen him do before.

"The court will take a fifteen minute recess," Judge Cass announced. The crowd of relatives filed out like sheep. I sat and rubbed Steve's shoulders and prayed, *Lord, help him. Help us all to know Your will.*

"How can I tell him what being a father means to me?" He choked out between sobs. "It means everything!" I held him and prayed, amazed at the depth of love in the man I married.

Fifteen minutes later, the judge returned along with the three lawyers and the others, now dead silent. "I'll deliver my decision by mail," he announced, then banged the gavel and said, "Court is adjourned."

That was it. *But what exactly happened?* We had no idea what the judge would decide. Steve worried that his tearful outburst had ruined everything, but I wondered. God had it all under His control. We'd have to wait.

Grandma Kidder and Aunt Marion had a wonderful day with our children, but were thoroughly exhausted when we finally picked them up at suppertime. "What's the baby's name?" Grandma asked.

"Bobby. Actually, it's Robert Edward Tonkin."

"What will you call him?"

"We'll call him Bobby. If the court gives him to us, we'll keep his whole name and just add Kidder at the end. It belongs to him."

"I had a Bob Kidder," she said wistfully, referring to Steve's dad, her firstborn. "Yes, that will be very nice, won't it?"

While we were away, our Vietnamese family finally moved into a home of their own. Amazing timing! Exhausted, we headed to Steve's sister Cindy and her husband Bob's home near Philadelphia to rest a few days and celebrate Thanksgiving together.

When we arrived home, a letter was waiting from the Chautauqua County Surrogate Court. The judge had made his decision allowing us to adopt Bobby. Hurray! We all leaped for joy! Christmas was on the way! We were to pick him up on December twenty-seventh, the day before David's third birthday.

With less than a month to prepare for Bobby's arrival, we hastily cleaned and painted the small bedroom the boys would now share, put up new curtains, and fitted in a crib, a changing table, and a double dresser. My mother babysat overnight while Steve and I drove back to Jamestown to pick up our new small son from the home of his aunt and uncle where he'd been staying. The doctor had given him a sedative for the trip, and he slept most of the ride home. Bobby's pale blond hair peeked out around the hood of his blue Winnie the Pooh winter coat as he slept.

Once or twice he woke up and sat still in the backseat of the car, staring at us. He was afraid to join us in the front seat. I wondered what he was thinking. How frightening it must be to be carried away by strangers after losing his parents and now leaving his siblings. I wanted to scoop him up into my arms and erase his hurts.

The children were waiting, sitting on the couch in their pajamas, as we carried a sleepy Bobby through the door to meet them. My mother, exhausted from two days of parenting, hugged him and hurried to her car to go home.

Instantly, Bobby reached out his arms to Lauren to pick him up. Amazed that anyone thought her responsible enough to do that, she hoisted him into her arms. Amy and David jumped up and down to squeeze his hand and give him a hug. Bobby never spoke a word, but smiled a weak little smile and sat on the couch to view his new world.

"Oh, he's so cute!"

The kids knelt down and patted his leg while I took off his blue coat.

"Look at his blue eyes!"

"Can I hold him again, Mommy?"

"I'll bet he wants a snack!"

The excitement escalated even more as Steve carried in the mountain of toys Bobby arrived with, lavish Christmas gifts from his aunts and uncles, brothers and sisters, and cousins.

Bob came equipped with more than just toys. He was cute, bright, full of energy, but over time, we also discovered he had an unbending will. If a line was drawn, Bob's toe crossed it. Whether it was eating breakfast or staying away from dangerous objects or coming when called, his little chin would go down to his chest as if to say, "You can't make me."

Our plan to absorb him into the family circle with a lot of love bridged many gaps, but not all. There was a place deep in Bobby's heart we couldn't reach.

We prayed constantly that God would give the love and bonding he needed. His answers come in strange ways. Bobby was sick a lot. When he was ill, he craved being held and rocked. I'd spend hours holding him in the black rocking chair. It made up for a lot of early cuddling we'd missed.

Then in late January, David developed severe croup, which landed him in the hospital in an oxygen tent. There he languished for a week with acute croup, pale and weak, with a cough that sounded like a party horn. Within days, all three children at home had it, too. Steve and I took turns caring for them, switching between the hospital and home day and night. Later, our pediatrician told us he wondered why he hadn't put all four children in one ward.

When it was finally over and everyone's horrible barking stopped, Steve and I had spent eight nights with barely any sleep other than small snatches here and there. Family bonding had begun. Bobby soon reached out to Steve and me for comfort and enjoyed being held like the other children.

Slowly but surely, God formed us into a new kind of family; not one without problems, but one that would learn in the coming years that grace, love, and forgiveness are the best gifts we ever give one another.

CHAPTER 10

Doused Hopes

He meant well.

I often remembered our friend Walt's parting prayer at our Bible study's send-off from Baltimore. He said, "Remember, even if God throws a bucket of cold water in your face, He still loves you."

"Oh, honey, don't tell them that!" his wife scolded. "Why burst their bubble?"

"Well, it's the truth! They might as well know it now."

Walt was right. We've been doused with lots of buckets of cold water over the years. I mean to talk to God about that one day.

Raising four kids has seasons of soaring joy, but also a fair share of catastrophes, emotional train wrecks, and financial draught. Add to that my repeated surgeries, twelve in all, for one stupid thing after another. I've been completely rebuilt. But several buckets of cold water made me wonder if God had turned away completely.

The first was David's bike accident when he was six. On Steve's birthday, while he and Amy rode their bikes around our circular street,

David thought he heard a car behind him. Instantly, he lost control and catapulted headfirst over the handlebars, smashing his face into the pavement. Amy ran for help and found our friends Sue and Ron, who were out working in their yard. She blurted out the news and then stopped breathing. Sue held her tight until her breathing came back, while Ron phoned us. Seconds later, we arrived at the devastating scene, finding David in a pool of blood, with another neighbor talking to him quietly. The shattered frame of David's glasses had broken into two jagged hooks that tore through his eyebrow and cheek, barely missing his eye, leaving two enormous holes filled with shards of glass in his small face.

Steve scooped David up and held him in the backseat while I drove to the hospital in a blur of tears. A plastic surgeon had just dealt with another emergency, and was instantly available. Amazing. A hundred stitches and many hours later, we arrived home with our heavily bandaged kindergartner, looking like a war victim.

It was hard not to show our alarm when looking at our beautiful son. We had to practice smiling and not looking at the wound. His sisters and brother were so kind, so gentle with him. Eventually, more plastic surgery and many years of healing smoothed David's face, giving him a ruggedly handsome appearance. But my trust in God would take longer to heal. My heart wrenched with grief. *Lord, why didn't You protect our son from such dreadful harm?*

Ten years later, we were doused again right before Lauren and Michael's wedding when Amy was diagnosed at seventeen with bipolar disorder. She was a faithful Christian in every way; yet, she endured mental tortures right out of the pit of darkness. The depth of her agony was unspeakably deep at times, causing her to cry out in emotional pain, wanting to die. Steve and I often held hands and cried at night. *Why, Lord? For what good reason did You allow this?*

During the same time span, our son Bob began an angry period of rebellion. One long sad night, Bob chose to leave home and spend his last year in high school living with his family in Jamestown. (You can read the whole story in my earlier book *Loving, Launching, and Letting Go*.) Steve drove him there, kissed him good-bye and unloaded his things, then drove 350 miles home all night. We both felt like complete failures as parents. *God, where are You? We need You!*

Two years later, as a new bride, Lauren was diagnosed with lupus, an autoimmune disease with serious health implications. I was in denial for a long time, terrified to face the truth. *Lord, not another dreadful illness! Lauren doesn't deserve this!*

I knew God loved His children and wanted the best for them, but I'd begun to wake each morning wondering, *What horrible thing are You going to allow today, Lord?*

I didn't have to wait long.

Steve seldom talked about his job. He'd grown accustomed to demanding bosses, difficult school superintendents, and the educational bureaucracy he served. I took his work for granted, like a backdrop for our lives that would just go on forever . . . until one Friday evening.

For months, Steve had been speaking around New York State demonstrating new learning technologies to school leaders. It was exhausting work. After the last event, he drove three hours home, arriving with a terrible headache. We had pizza and the usual family shenanigans. I noticed Steve was quieter than normal.

Around 6:30 Saturday morning, I found him sitting hunched forward on the living room sofa, wearing a hat and trench coat.

"What are you doing with a hat and coat on?" I asked. It was certainly not cold.

"I've been up all night. Call the doctor and then take me to the hospital."

"What's wrong?"

"Something really bad. I don't know." Steve never said things like that. I rushed to call Dr. Mastroianni, grabbed my car keys, and scribbled a quick note to our teenagers. Steve walked slowly to the car, easing himself in the seat laboriously. *He's never sick! What on earth could this be—the flu?*

Nothing happens quickly in an emergency room, except that Steve was clearly so ill he couldn't sit upright. I had to make noise.

"We need help here! Fast! Please get someone out here!" It worked. Steve was lifted onto a gurney and placed in a cubicle right away. There we waited for hours while doctors handled other emergencies. Drops of sweat beaded on his forehead. I only had to touch him to know he was burning up with fever. Suddenly, Steve curled into a ball, groaning with pain. I became frantic for help to come, but it was nowhere in sight.

Just then a close friend from church arrived. After listening in earnest as I downloaded my frustration, he said with some authority, "I've got friends in this hospital," and disappeared around the curtain. Minutes later, doctors appeared to examine Steve and order a CT scan. When he came back, he was given a quiet place to rest in a locker room/storage space near the ER.

Nearly nine hours after we'd arrived, a doctor called me into the hall and said, "Your husband either has an aneurism or meningitis. Both are very serious. Unfortunately, we don't know yet which it is. We need permission to do a spinal tap."

A spinal tap? This was no flu. *Is this real, Lord? Where are You? We need You!*

"Of course. Do what you have to do! Can you give him anything for his pain?"

"Unfortunately, not until we know."

By now, Steve's face was contorted with pain. He moaned and groaned and perspired heavily, unable to move. Two doctors arrived to perform the spinal tap; one was a resident who accidentally hit a nerve, sending Steve into even more painful spasms. The other quickly took over.

It was clearly meningitis, but would take twelve more hours before they knew whether it was viral or bacterial; the latter usually proved deadly. Terror gripped me. Was it possible Steve could die this quickly? *Are you there, Lord? Why don't You DO something?*

Steve was placed on a floor in isolation near the nurse's station and finally given pain medication. I had to "gown up" and not touch Steve or anything in the room. Just sit and wait.

There we sat, one deathly ill husband and one cotton-clad wife, waiting for encouragement from a God who had seemed silent and powerless far too long. I tried to pray, but couldn't. All I could say was, "I love you, Steve. I love you." I couldn't even hold his hand.

Later that night I drove home to see the kids. Someone fixed glasses of milk and toast and peanut butter, our favorite soul food. I shared the details with them about the two kinds of meningitis and the twelve-hour wait. The kids all hugged me and said, "We're praying Mom. Don't worry. God will take care of Dad."

I couldn't tell them my worst fear was that He wouldn't.

Steve had asked me to try to get some sleep, which seemed impossible at first, but I conked out the moment I lay down.

It seemed like only an instant later when the phone woke me up. I looked at the clock. It was 6:30 in the morning. *Oh, my gosh! I've slept all night! Steve! How is he?* By the time I said, "Hello," I was certain it was bad news.

"Is this Mrs. Kidder?"

"Yes."

"This is St. Clare's Hospital, Mrs. Kidder. We're calling to tell you Steve's tests just came back. He has viral meningitis, not bacterial."

"Oh, thank God! Thank God! I'll be over very soon."

"There's no rush. He's finally sleeping. We just gave him more pain medication."

I sat on the edge of the bed and sighed deeply. *What did I just say? Thank God?* Then I fell to my knees, aware for the first time in a long time that God was right there with me.

Oh, Father! Forgive me for not trusting You! Forgive me for all my doubts about Your love and goodness. Thank You so much for rescuing Steve from this deadly illness. Lord, I've grown so fearful of Your will, of what You've allowed. I may never understand why, but please give me peace right now to rest Steve in Your arms. Heal him, Lord. Please heal him fully. Thank You ahead of time. In Jesus' name, amen.

It was a turning point for me. Gradually, God helped me trust Him with our children's struggles, with the outcomes of their choices and the adversities we all face from time to time. He helped me see that His greater plan includes both good things and bad. We do live on a spiritual battlefield. Being wounded is part of belonging to Him. I had a lot to learn.

One morning a few months later, I sat alone with my Bible open to Psalm 103. I read each verse slowly, asking God, *Father, is this true for me, too?*

Yes, my soul could praise the Lord and "forget not all his benefits" (v. 2) with the psalmist now. God had done just what He said He would: Forgive my sins, heal all my diseases, redeem my life from the pit, and crown me with love and compassion (see vv. 3–4). I deserved none of it. Yes, He did "[satisfy my] desires with good things so that [my] youth is renewed like the eagle's" (v. 5).

Best of all, Steve was now the picture of health again. Our kids were learning to handle the challenges God had allowed each one. I still felt deep pain over what each one suffered, but I had to admit that things were improving.

Then I came to the following verses and stopped: "The Lord is compassionate and gracious, slow to anger, abounding in love. He will not always accuse, nor will he harbor his anger forever; he does not treat us as our sins deserve or repay us according to our iniquities. For as high as the heavens are above the earth, so great is his love for those who fear him; as far as the east is from the west, so far has he removed our transgressions from us. As a father has compassion on his children, so the Lord has compassion on those who fear him" (Psalm 103:8–13). This was the most personal part. My Father was talking to me, His child. Though I deserved nothing, He had given me everything.

Thank You, Lord, for letting me see a little better who You really are! You are worthy to be praised. I can thank You now for Your steadfast love, Your compassion and mercies even when I don't understand. Lord, when I feel doubts, please help me remember to take them to You right away so they won't take root in my heart again. Please give me a happy heart, a thankful and trusting heart all over again, better than before. In Jesus' strong name, amen.

Our friend was right. Even when God allows a bucket of cold water in our face, He still loves us and His nature has not changed. I can trust Him to dry me off and walk me through the mess.

CHAPTER 11

A Small Miracle

L ike many others do, our family did normal in high gear. "Can somebody set the table?" My voice went up an octave. "Now?"

"Mom, can you hurry dinner?" Lauren dumped her backpack on a living room chair and peeked in the kitchen. "I've got a concert rehearsal in a half hour and I need you to drive me."

"I'm kind of busy, honey. Maybe Dad can. He'll be here in a minute."

"But I have to be there on time, Mom! Mrs. Lewis will kill me if I'm late!" *Why is everything an emergency to a fifteen-year-old?*

"Okay. We'll get you there," I said, glancing over my shoulder at an empty table. "Amy, isn't it your turn to set the table? Let's get moving, honey. Dinner will be ready any minute."

"Just one more minute, Mom. Pleeeze?" It seemed cruel to tear a fifth grader away from *Little House on the Prairie*.

Steve walked in the garage door just as Amy jumped up and came in the kitchen. "Oh, hi, Dad!" She ran to give him a big hug. Bob and Dave looked up from their spot on the floor in front of the television. "Hey, Dad!"

"Hi, kids." Steve tried to act happy, but his body said otherwise. I saw tension in his jaw once again. His job had grown in the past two years, causing him to be extra busy. He'd also been named chairman of the elder board at church. An extended pulpit search for a new pastor had resulted in many late night meetings. There was pressure from the congregation to "get it done," yet they'd already turned down several candidates. He was weary and it showed.

"Hi, honey." I stopped cooking briefly to give him a kiss. "Shepherd's pie is almost ready. Are you hungry?"

"Starved."

"Good! Dinner in two minutes. Kids, turn off the television, wash your hands, and come to the table!" I took the casserole and warm rolls from the oven. The aroma filled the room.

Just as we were sitting down, the phone rang. "Tell whoever it is we'll call them back," I said, adding, "even if it's the president."

We joined hands as Steve gave thanks for our food. "Remember to pass to the right, kids. Wait your turn, boys," he coached.

"*Mom.*" Lauren looked anguished, holding up her watch. "I've got to be there in *ten minutes!*"

"We'll leave right after dinner. I promise."

Big sighs from across the table. I looked at Steve and wondered, *Is this the best we can do with family life? We need help!*

Grabbing my car keys a few minutes later, I rushed out the door to transport Lauren and her cello to school. Poor kid. She knew I was annoyed. It wasn't her fault.

Life accelerated daily as each of our four kids became steeped in sports or music, youth group, and plans with their friends. I spent my days keeping our lives on track, chauffeuring, cooking, and doing laundry. Steve and I both led ministries at church that required plenty of time and attention. Other people seemed to manage. We could, too, I supposed.

One day I noticed we'd all stopped smiling. Big surprise. The kids squabbled more; I was growing irritable from carpooling, sometimes a hundred miles a day, and running behind on household work. Unwinding our busy lives seemed impossible. Must have been God was listening.

My mother called one morning, pumped with excitement. "I just had my hair done and my hairdresser's friend is selling Yorkshire terrier puppies! I'm going to go look at them this afternoon. Want to come?"

"You bet! What time?" I'd loved Yorkies since I was a little girl and my Aunt Ginny had one. They were yappy but adorable, smart and loyal to a fault. This would make Mother so happy since her dog had died recently. My mother loved dogs almost more than people.

"Is three okay? I'll pick you up. Bring the kids. They'll love seeing the puppies."

We arrived at the two-hundred-year-old farmhouse just as a goat walked out of the barn to greet us. "Oh, look, kids! There's a goat! I hope he's safe." Thankfully Margaret, its owner, emerged smiling on the back porch and walked over to the car.

"Don't mind him." She spoke with a British accent. "He's an old bloke. Wouldn't harm a flea. Come inside and see my pups."

Maxine, a beautiful but feisty Yorkie mom, laid in her bed in the kitchen nursing three little black balls of fluff. "Oh, how cute! Look, kids!" I bent down for a closer view.

"Don't touch her!" Margaret cautioned loudly. "She'll bite your hand off! She's very protective of those pups. I'll have to move her to let you see them." We all stepped aside to give Maxine plenty of room as

Margaret gently pushed the pups away and swung the growling mama onto a bed in the next room, shutting the door tightly. "There's a little boy and two girls. I'm keeping one of the girls."

Mother picked up the little boy pup, cuddling him close to her face. It was love at first sight. Amy, Dave, and Bob knelt down and gently stroked the silky fur of the other two puppies. Their tiny button noses, pink tongues, and beautiful dark eyes gave the impression of living stuffed animals. We were captivated.

"I'm goin' into the hospital soon," Margaret said. "And it won't be fun, if you know what I mean. This is serious. I have to place my pups in loving homes before that. If you want one, I'll give it to you half price."

Mother was elated. Imagine having a new Yorkie puppy in the family! "When will they be ready to leave their mom?" Mother asked.

"Three weeks. Leave your number and I'll call you." Mother wrote out a check, put her phone number on it, and drove us straight to Burger King. It was time for a party!

In three weeks, when her puppy was ready, Steve arranged to leave work early and pick Lauren up from school, then rendezvous with us at Mother's house. What the children didn't know, and I learned only that morning, was that Steve had also purchased the little girl dog for our family. When we placed Mother's puppy into a soft bed on the floor of the car, I carried his little sister out to join him.

"Mommy, what are you doing? Are you taking that dog?"

"No, honey, this is a surprise gift from your Dad. What do you think of that?" Their whoops of joy were deafening.

When we arrived at Mother's house, Steve and Lauren were waiting. Soon we all lay on our stomachs in the grass watching our black silky pups roll and play together. We named them Charlie and Laidy (pronounced with a cockney accent), after Prince Charles and Lady Diana.

I glanced up and saw Steve smiling; no, he was grinning and laughing. Mother seemed to be ten years younger. Had I ever seen her have this much fun? Suddenly, we were all children again, captivated by our adorable twin puppies who soon took over our lives and our hearts.

Mother's life was transformed, really consumed, with the fun she had with them. Whenever we were away, she babysat Laidy so the two dogs could play together, and bounce along shoulder to shoulder on their long red leashes. She even took them in the car for ice cream cones.

Laughter and smiles became Laidy's daily gifts to our family, but that wasn't all. Though only five pounds, she had a ferocious bark that kept strangers at bay, especially men, and even other dogs. She once terrified a neighbor's visiting bloodhound, sending him howling out of our yard. The pizza deliveryman wouldn't set foot in our house. The only men she loved were Steve, and of course, our sons. That was about it.

Laidy was a champion at daily entertainment, dodging everyone's attempts to grab a toy bone from her mouth, and guarding her toys, my shoes, and my Bible like they were her babies. When we had a party, she could navigate a crowded room without getting stepped on, ducking around feet like a magician.

An accomplished snack thief, Laidy regularly stole from lunch bags left on the living room chair before school. And when anyone asked, "Laidy, do you want a bath?" she'd slink upstairs and pretend to be invisible. She was so smart that we finally had to spell out words when we didn't want her to know what we were saying.

One of the funniest things about Laidy was her smile. Especially when Steve or the children came in the front door, she curled back her lips and let all her teeth show in a real smile. That had to be a reflection of God's sense of humor.

Laidy came to us right when we needed her. A gift of love from

Steve to the family, she was one of God's good and perfect gifts that came down from heaven. And why not? Doesn't our Creator love to shower His children with good gifts? What better than a daily reminder that life is more important than work, or duty, or our schedules? It's about love, in this case from a Father to His children.

For eleven years, Laidy's faithful love and funny personality taught us to lighten up and not take ourselves too seriously. She never left the front windows when we were away, waiting for hours on the back of the living room chair. Whenever we pulled in the driveway, the car lights caught the outline of her little ears in the window. I still miss them.

One by one the children all left home for college, leaving just the three of us: Steve, Laidy, and me. She slept more, sometimes all day, and tired quickly on walks around the block. I had to carry her home often. The day Laidy died, she held on all day until evening. I bathed her to cool her fevered body and trimmed some of her long fur to make her more comfortable. Around five thirty, when she heard the sound of Steve's voice, she rose laboriously from her corner in our bedroom, walked slowly sideways into the upstairs hall and smiled at him, one last time. We both knew her mission was complete.

CHAPTER 12

Single File

I've never had a vision. Well, maybe one. Some might say it was a dream or a hallucination. I'm not sure, but I know I was dying and Jesus came for me. The experience changed me profoundly.

It happened on a bitterly cold weekend one January. Our dear friends Gordon and Lorraine Tucker offered us their vacation home in the Adirondack Mountains for a little break. With our exchange student Alejandra visiting from Guatemala and Lauren home from college watching the home front, it seemed fine to leave.

Steve and I piled on our warmest clothes and loaded a cooler full of food into the van and headed west on the New York State Thruway. Just as we turned north through Amsterdam, snowflakes began to fall.

"I didn't think we were supposed to get snow this weekend. Did you?" I asked, wiping mist off the inside of the windshield.

"You never know what you'll find in the mountains. This van can handle anything." He looked over at me and grinned. "Not to worry!"

The Adirondacks are wild and remote in the winter. I watched the snowdrifts grow higher and higher as we pressed past the dense woods. Gusts of wind blew snow across the road in wide white stripes.

"Are we almost there?"

"Another half hour or less."

I closed my eyes and put my head back, thinking how good it felt to get away from everything for a couple of days. We needed this break.

The narrow dirt road around the lake wasn't fully plowed, so we parked about fifty yards from the camp and walked in, hauling our duffel bags and cooler through the snow. We arrived at the camp a few minutes later just as the late afternoon sun lowered in the sky.

"It gets dark earlier in the mountains, doesn't it?"

"Sure does. I'd better turn on the heat and get a fire started," Steve said.

"I'll unpack the food and see about dinner." An hour later we ate by candlelight, snuggled together in front of the wide stone fireplace. Snow swirled outside the massive picture windows and sealed us in from the dark outside world. The crackling flames spelled warmth and romance. *Dreams are made of nights like this! Oh, thank You, God! I'm so happy!*

Saturday morning we went cross-country skiing, shuffling and sliding through the fresh snow. The wind blew large white clumps off the trees onto our heads and down our backs. We laughed and fell down, then stood and listened to the silence of our wooded sanctuary. The day was perfect from start to finish. It wasn't until that night that something happened.

Around three o'clock in the morning, I awoke with searing pain in the middle of my back. Trying not to disturb Steve, I took my pillow and an extra blanket and headed for the living room sofa. The embers still glowed in the fireplace, but nothing brought comfort. I searched through the bathroom cupboard until at last I found ibuprofen tablets and took a couple. In the morning, Steve found me on the couch shivering violently.

"What's wrong? Are you cold?" He switched on the light, then bent down closer. "You're all covered with spots!"

"I am?" I looked at my arms and saw a mass of little red dots. Steve looked at my back. Same spots. I was covered.

"Do you feel sick?"

"Not really sick, but my back is killing me."

"Did you eat anything unusual?"

"Just what you ate. Oh, but I did finish up my prescription for that bladder infection. It was sulfa something."

"We'd better leave as soon as it's daylight. I'll get the fire going again and make some coffee."

It must have snowed all night. Steve had to push the back door open. Had I felt better, staying another day would have been a dream. Now, I wondered how we'd even get to the car. But Steve managed to pull all our belongings out on a sled, helping me through the snow to a warm, waiting car a little while later.

The main roads were plowed and salted making the trip home an easy one with no stops along the way. Lauren and Alejandra and the gang were at church, so Steve bundled me up in bed with an extra blanket or two and a hot cup of tea. I still couldn't stop shivering. "Can you take a little nap?" he said. "I have an elders' meeting, but I'll come right back. Promise." Neither of us realized danger was imminent.

Sometime later I wandered downstairs, feeling weak. The children were home now, taking naps, except David, who was watching a television show by himself. "Hi, Mom. How do you feel? Dad said you were sick."

"Cold, Dave. Can you make a fire?"

"Sure, Mom. You okay?" He quickly set the logs in place in our woodstove, closed the vents on the back, and began rolling newspapers. That's when I realized I was losing consciousness.

"Call Lauren . . . need to go to hospital."

"Mom! Stay right there!" David moved fast.

When I opened my eyes next, both Lauren and Amy had their coats on and were ready to go. The problem was, it was now sixteen below zero, and I was already freezing. I heard Lauren say, "Get her a quilt. I'll start the car." It never occurred to any of us to call an ambulance.

I have a vague memory of the ambulance entrance at the hospital, car doors slamming, and Lauren and Amy half carrying me inside. Two nurses hoisted me onto a gurney and wheeled me to a space behind a curtain, chatting nonsense all the way. "So what's your name? When were you born? Can you tell me what day this is?" I struggled to answer, but my mouth wasn't working right. My spots spoke for me. "Have you been on any new medication, Mrs. Kidder?"

"Sulfa."

That's when the room went away and Jesus walked in.

He walked right toward me, His head thrown back with a warm smile. *Come!* He said, offering His hand. Behind Him lay a narrow path, much like a garden path, curving toward an ancient gate made of wood, rounded on top. Through the cracks, light streamed from behind it. I knew this must be heaven's door.

Jesus motioned for me to follow Him, but I hung back, afraid. Bordering the path to the left was deep darkness, the kind that terrified me as a child. I'd look under the bed and feel around in the closet, certain a monster waited to harm me. I grabbed Jesus' hand tightly, and walked closely behind Him, suddenly aware that my hospital Johnny was flapping wide open behind me. His hand in mine was warm and strong.

Come and see what you've been afraid of all your life. Jesus looked toward the darkness. I could see clearly in the Light that shown from

Him that a monster was there, all right, but he was a toothless, washed-up dragon. A joke! *This is Death,* He said. *But you have nothing to fear. He has no power over you when I'm holding your hand.*

Instantly, I relaxed. Looking Death in the face was easy! Nothing to it! "But, Lord," a new consideration make me ask, "what about those who aren't holding Your hand?"

They have much to fear. His tone was grave and sad. I looked at the hand that held mine. It was pierced and bloodstained. *The cross! That's why! Without Jesus' death on the cross, I'd be alone in the darkness forever, facing Death all alone.* He smiled, knowing I finally understood.

"Am I dying, Lord?" I asked, now unafraid. I wanted Him to take me beyond the gate. Home.

Not yet, He smiled. *You have more loving to do.*

Just then, my two chatty nurses arrived with a large hypodermic needle. "Here, darlin.' You're in anaphylactic shock, but this shot of Benadryl will fix you up soon. Here's another blanket." I wanted to thank them, but couldn't form the words. "Your daughters want to see you. I'll bring them back in a few moments."

I lay on the gurney and stared at the holes in the ceiling. *What just happened to me, Lord? I know You are here and I'm not dead. You have more loving for me to do? I wonder what You meant by that?*

"Oh, Mom!" Lauren and Amy appeared, still in their down coats. "We've been so worried about you. We called Dad and he's on the way." I smiled but couldn't talk yet. My girls looked so beautiful to me, so strong and brave.

Steve arrived and the nurses asked the girls to wait outside again, assuring them I'd be fine. "Maybe you'd better go home and be with Dave and Bob. I'll stay with Mom now," he said. Reluctantly, they kissed me good-bye, squeezed my hand, and left.

Steve sat by my bed and held my hand gently. "Don't try to talk now," he said. "Just rest. Everything will be all right. I'll stay right here."

I wanted to tell him something wonderful just happened. I'd seen heaven's gate, felt Jesus' nail-pierced hand in mine, and finally understood His triumph over Death. And I knew, just knew, I'd never fear Death again.

The cross now loomed large and victorious across the stretch of eternity. The narrow path to heaven's door was only wide enough for One. Walking single file, holding Jesus' hand, we are forever safe. Staying close was what mattered.

I'd never felt homesick for heaven before, but sometimes I long to see the other side of the gate. At just the right time, Jesus will come for me, as He will for each child of God.

In the hospital, nurses sat with me around the clock for the first two nights. After a week, I was finally sent home. By now my spots blurred together, looking like a king-sized sunburn. I felt weak, but peaceful.

When I told my family about my experience at heaven's door, they believed me, but couldn't process the reality that I'd nearly died. That was okay. One day David handed me a drawing he'd made, saying, "Is this what it looked like, Mom?"

"Exactly! How did you do that?"

"I just closed my eyes and imagined what you described."

That happened in 1988. I've rarely told this story. After all, it was only one little vision, and a quick one at that. I'm still very much alive, and now understand what Jesus meant about having "more loving to do." I'm glad I didn't know it would stretch me so much. But it did. Loving is the most important work any of us will ever do, and it's seldom easy. Only God's grace gives us the love for others we need, but it's the best reason there is to get up every morning. And the only way the world, and those we love, will ever know God is real.

CHAPTER 13

Love Banquet Style

O h no! Not company!"

I groaned out loud the moment my car rounded the corner and our house came into full view. Normally I'd be thrilled to see four cars lined up in our driveway, but after a weeklong vigil at the hospital with a very ill child, I knew my house would be a colossal mess. "Oh well, who cares?" None of it seemed important now. Turning off the engine, I dragged up to the front door to face the music.

"What are you doing home so soon?" my friend Judie called from the kitchen. "We weren't expecting you for another hour! We thought we'd be long gone by then." She walked toward me with a huge hug, then added softly, "How are you doin', girl?" *Was this my house? Was I dreaming? Everything looked so good. Where did these flowers come from?*

Suddenly, more voices, more hugs. Lorraine, smiling and wiping beads of perspiration from her forehead, came up from the family room where she had just finished my entire mountain of ironing and done all our laundry. Regina peeked into the kitchen with a little giggle, having vacuumed, polished, and dusted every room in the house. Joan, still up-stairs wrestling with the boys' bunk bed sheets, called down her hello, having brought order out of the sheer chaos into each of our bedrooms.

"When did you guys get here?" I plopped down exhausted on a kitchen chair. It was my last coherent sentence. Once the tears came, they came in great heaving waves. "How come . . . how come . . . you did all this?" I cried unashamedly, every ounce of resistance gone. We had spent a week praying through a health crisis, begging God for a sense of His presence at the hospital. And He responded by arranging for a mantle of order, beauty, and loving care into our home through these four angels.

"Don't you worry about anything," Lorraine said firmly. "Here's tonight's dinner and there are more meals in the freezer." The table was set with flowers and fancy napkins, a little gift at my place. Arranged on the stove was a banquet, complete with salad and dessert in the fridge.

"You rest awhile now, Virelle. We're all praying. God has everything under control. Don't you worry." One by one, my four friends left as quickly as they had come. I wandered from room to room, still sobbing from the enormity of their gift. *They must have picked every flower in their gardens!* I thought, finding beautiful arrangements in every room. *And what's this?* Little wrapped gifts on each bed. More tears.

It was in the living room I found their small note under the vase of peonies. I was to have come home and found it as their only signature. Will I ever forget the words? Not even when I'm an old lady. "The Love Squad[1] was here."

In creative and sacrificial ways, Christian friends like those in the "Love Squad" have lavished me with living examples of my heavenly Father's love. Once my friend Doris drove to my house in an ice storm to bring our family a Winter Carnival Casserole.

"Why did you do this?" I asked, stunned by her gift.

"I remember what it felt like to feed four children every night," she said with a smile. A meal for no reason? That's love. In an ice storm? Hard to fathom.

These friends made giving look easy, but it's not. Giving love takes a surrendered schedule, a willing heart, and costs way more than first imagined. My small acts of service paled in comparison to others who have given pooped-out caregivers a reprieve, huffed and puffed alongside single moms in labor, given cars, paid off debt for another in hard times, or housed someone else's rebel, as several of our friends did for us. There's no measure on earth for such love. It's impossible to repay, except by our willingness to also give as God directs.

I have only to look at Jesus to trace the pattern. But His pattern is so different from mine. When I think of giving love banquet style, cooking a holiday feast is my first thought. I want to invite my family and friends, plus one or two others with no place to go. Entertaining revs me up. Even when I'm asleep, I often dream of table settings, centerpieces, and recipes—something Steve finds really strange.

Why not? Jesus loved a good party. I love that about Him! But His guest list was way different from mine. Once He said to His host, "When you give a luncheon or dinner, do not invite your friends, your brothers or relatives, or your rich neighbors; if you do, they may invite you back and so you will be repaid. But when you give a banquet, invite the poor, the crippled, the lame, the blind, and you will be blessed" (Luke 14:12–14a). When I read this, my first thought was, "But that takes all the fun out of it! I love entertaining my family and friends."

Jesus read my mind and guided me to see things His way a moment. Was *I* not once spiritually blind, crippled by sin's effects? When Steve and I were broken with sorrow, did others not soothe our spirits with homemade soup at their table, and offer to walk with us through our pain? Had I not been the poor one, also? Many times. I felt a wave of shame.

Lord, I've been so needy at points throughout my life. Your faithful ones welcomed me to a banquet of undeserved service and love. I see what You mean now. Direct me, Lord. I want to serve those You invite into our lives. Oh, forgive me for being so self-serving and small when You wanted me to extend Your great "Welcome Home!" banquet to those You love.

Thanks to a parade of obedient givers, I have a better idea now how to do that.

Note

1. "The Love Squad" was first published in *Decision* magazine (October, 1999) and has since been published in many collected works.

CHAPTER 14

Learning to Sit Still

M om, we're going to be late for Sunday school! Mrs. Parker will kill me!"

"She won't kill you, honey. This is church. Dad'll be out in a minute," I assured my ten-year-old son, checking my watch one more time. Now we had only fifteen minutes left for a seventeen-minute trip. *Why can't he get ready on time?*

Steve was a champion at last-minute appearances. A man born without the benefit of an inner clock, he'd do all the breakfast dishes, empty the trash, or check the dryer before getting dressed. He still does. Just when I'd be ready to explode, he would swing out the front door carrying his Bible, smiling like nothing was wrong. The Kidders were five minutes late to everything.

In my home growing up, being late was a mortal sin. But Steve, the middle of six children, learned to express love by doing one more thing to help, all at the same deliberate pace. In over forty years of marriage, I've seen him hurry fewer than ten times.

I am his polar opposite. Being even a smidgen late gives me acid indigestion and a wild urge to make up excuses: "There must have been an accident on the freeway—traffic was at a standstill" or "My watch must be running late." It's been an ongoing source of conflict. Imagine my horror when I realized God does things just like Steve.

For one, He does nothing on command. When faced with a pressing need, I've tried praying authoritatively, using Jesus' name, in confidence, fully believing that what I asked for would happen. Like right now. But it didn't. Often what followed was a long period of silence, dragging doubt and disappointment on its heels. Sometimes, God answers fast. Why not every time? Didn't Jesus say, "I tell you the truth, if anyone says to this mountain, 'Go throw yourself into the sea,' and does not doubt in his heart but believes that what he says will happen, it will be done for him'?" (Mark 11: 23). He did, but unfortunately, He never mentioned when.

It was the same with my husband. I learned early in our marriage that Steve switches into slow motion, if any at all, when I say something like, "The garage needs cleaning" or "Be sure you write so-and-so." At first I thought he was pretending not to hear me. He'd look the other way acting as though I hadn't said anything. So I'd turn up the volume a tad, prefacing it with, "You know, the garage is a mess." He'd agree it certainly needed cleaning, but when nothing happened, I'd feel hurt, angry, and disappointed.

It's not that Steve is lazy. *Au contraire*, he's a fabulous worker, and full of surprises. Once I pulled in the driveway on Mother's Day weekend to discover he'd cleared out a tough network of tree roots from a large corner of our wooded lot and planted a coveted raspberry patch in my honor. Every July those hardy bushes kept us in delicious raspberry jam for another year.

And that's not all. Every one of our four children knows how to keep a house clean, not because of my great example. They've watched their dad help with laundry, vacuuming, and dishes since they were small, just like Steve's dad helped. The list is endless. So why does Steve shut down when I use my "this-is-what-needs-doing-now" tone?

Possibly because it's not nice. Or respectful. In fact, I wouldn't like it either. Apparently, neither does God. It's taken far too long for me to realize that love seldom uses a demanding tone unless it's training a puppy. (Maybe not even then.) Loving people learn to ask, not demand. And then wait quietly, the litmus test of trust for anyone like me.

Words float back to me from years ago. Sitting in the living room of friends from Baltimore, our Bible study leader spoke of the way his life was changed by Isaiah 30:15: "In repentance and rest is your salvation, in quietness and trust is your strength." Through a long period of financial reversals, he'd learned to wait on God with a quiet attitude, trusting Him to work things out in His own good time. It struck me that's usually how God builds leaders.

"Wait, my daughter," Naomi spoke to her treasured daughter-in-law (Ruth 3:18). How many times has God said that to me? But Ruth didn't chafe or argue. She simply waited, trusting Naomi's wisdom, her faith, her God. Quietness and confidence became her great strength. And God answered way beyond the best dream she'd ever had. (If you need a soul-sweeping romance, read the whole book of Ruth. It may be short, but it will knock your socks off.)

Many long waits feel like pregnancy. There's a happy ending in sight—a new baby to love, the promise of good things on the horizon. That's the kind I like. Anticipated joys fuel hope and expectancy. There's an end in sight, and a good one at that.

But every wait doesn't have a rainbow. Some have a question mark, or worse, a feared cliff. I asked Steve today what were the toughest waiting periods we've had. Thoughtful a long time, as usual, he finally answered, "Probably waiting for loved ones to come to Christ."

"That's true. Some did, but we're still waiting for many others."

"How about all the times my promotions at the state were derailed?" Steve referred to many dragged-out disappointments working for a bureaucracy that changed with the speed of an iceberg.

"The worst times for me were waiting for kids to drive home at night in bad weather! Remember those days?"

"Don't remind me. How about waiting for medication to work when they were sick?"

"Like the time David had acute croup in the hospital and the other three had bronchitis and croup at home. I thought we'd never live through it."

There've been many long waits to be sure, some far more serious than others, with no happy ending in sight. Health issues are especially hard. In my early thirties and forties, I found myself in Albany Medical Center regularly, usually to have cysts in my wrists or feet removed, or for carpal tunnel surgery, or fibrocystic disease in my breasts. In fact, I spent four birthdays in a row there. Strangely, I never worried about cancer until one dreary spring when my doctor found another lump on my right breast. *Here we go again*, I thought.

"You have too much fibrocystic disease, Virelle," he said as I lay on the examining table. "Instead of excising just the lump, I recommend a simple mastectomy. There's no healthy breast tissue here at all."

I couldn't believe my ears. "A mastectomy? Are you sure?" I was only thirty-three.

"A plastic surgeon could remove all the breast tissue and replace it with an implant."

Tears came to my eyes. "I'm sorry. I wasn't prepared for that."

The doctor sighed heavily and patted my hand kindly. "I'll tell you what. Let's do one more lumpectomy. Then, if there's a next time, we'll do the mastectomy. Talk it over with your husband."

Numbly, I dressed and left the office. A half hour later I stood at a pay phone in a nearby bank, sobbing the news to Steve.

"I think you should have the mastectomy now," he said softly. "I don't want to lose you."

"No. No. Just one more time," I rambled between deep, heaving sobs. "I'll wait one more time."

"I'll come home now. Stay where you are. I'll pick you up."

"No. I can drive. Just give me a few minutes. I'll meet you home in half an hour."

The lumpectomy was done as an outpatient procedure this time. Even though it was benign, I still cried during the night through most of May, dreading the next time. Steve often held me and whispered, "It'll be all right. We'll make it through this. God will take us through."

I waited for pain: checked when in the shower for another lump, wondering what changes an implant would bring and wrestled with a morbid sense of bravery at all costs. A close friend, who knew my situation, called one day with verses from Psalm 94 to encourage me: "When I said, 'My foot is slipping,' your love, O Lord, supported me. When anxiety was great within me, your consolation brought joy to my soul" (vv.18–19). I waited for consolation. And I waited.

One hot Sunday afternoon in mid-August while the family napped after church, I felt the need to pray alone. Tiptoeing down the stairs, I knelt by the couch, quietly reflecting on a comment I'd heard that morning in Sunday school. Someone said in class, "God allows only what's best for us." *Lord, is that true? Are You telling me a mastectomy is best for me? Because it doesn't sound good at all.*

I had no direct answer from the Lord, just quietness. I thought a long time about how many good gifts God had already given: we were both believers by some miracle of grace, our four children had each

invited Christ into their hearts at age four—amazing! I had every blessing I could want, except the sturdy health I longed for. *Would God deal
capriciously with me now?* No. He would not.

In a silent exchange, I gave Him my will on the matter. *You choose
what's best for me, Lord. If a mastectomy is it, that's okay with me. I thank
You for it now.*

That was it. No great revelation. Just quietness. Confidence. Peace
within. No matter what happened, I felt certain God would do what
was best for me.

Summer faded into autumn, crimson and gold. The children went
off to school. In late September I had another appointment with my
doctor, fully expecting to set the date for my surgery.

"Well, you're fine," he said after examining me. "See you in a year."

"What do you mean? I don't need a mastectomy now?"

"Why would you? There's no new lump."

No new lump. I dressed in a fog.

Facing the brilliant afternoon sun, I stepped off the office porch
and walked to my car. *Is this it, Lord? No mastectomy is what's best for
me? Imagine that! And I was all prepared for it, too! Well, thank You!
Thank You!* I couldn't wait to tell Steve.

It's been years since then. Every year I feel grateful for renewed
health. Sure, there have been other issues, other surgeries, but each
time I'm certain God is in control and He only allows what's best for
me. I can pray better for others who wait, apprehensive and fearful. I
know how that feels.

So what is God looking for? It's taken me decades to realize that
waiting is more a posture of the heart than tapping my foot over the
passage of time. It's willingness to yield to the One who loves me most,
bowing to His Lordship—a requirement for learning anything deeper
about God. Always open to our cry, the King of heaven is never in a

hurry and expects to be trusted. His answers are always best, perfectly on time, and are worlds better than anything I could have imagined on my own.

Our kids are grown now. Rarely does Steve keep me waiting anymore. We finally learned to build margins around our life that offered more flexibility and less rush. I've also learned more about waiting quietly and asking nicely. Big lessons, seldom easy for anyone.

We have friends who wait today while cancer's tentacles claim a spouse, or a tumor expands inside a son-in-law's head, or a beloved child changes course in sexual orientation or waits in a prison cell. What are they to do? How does any child of God wait quietly while the guillotine seems poised above?

Perhaps by grace. Perhaps by exhausting every repentant thought, every prayer for change. Then what remains is to lay our head on His lap and rest in His care. "Though he slay me, yet will I hope in him," said Job at a similar moment (13:15). Only by grace is quietness and confidence our strength—and only when His strange and holy Presence takes over completely. Such submission is not learned in seasons of blessing, but when every alternative is gone, we find He is enough, and His way is best.

CHAPTER 15

"Climbing

on the Altar"

"What's for supper, Mom? Smells great in here!"
"Something special! Wait and see."

Who doesn't love to walk into the house and sniff something yummy? Different smells mean different things. On a cold day, a roast in the oven means company's coming! And hamburgers or hot dogs on the grill in summer, homemade pizza, chocolate chip cookies, even popcorn in the microwave, all smell like family fun. Some days it's the only thing that makes you feel loved.

Giving love takes endless forms. Edith Schaeffer knew that flowers on the table, a clean bathroom, even clean sheets could send a powerful message that someone cares about you a lot. I once read about a runaway teenaged girl, steeped in shame from layers of poor choices, who was offered a bed to sleep on that had clean sheets. Nestling into the pillow, feeling the crisp sheets on her exhausted body, she remembered sleeping in her grandmother's home as a little girl. Her grandmother loved Jesus and prayed with her often. Drifting to sleep, her heart cried out, "Help me, Jesus!" Tears of repentance covered the sweet-smelling pillow, and she turned a corner in her life that day.

I've met people whose lives are like those sheets.

After years without knowing Christ personally, I came into the family of God at age twenty-five. Steve followed two years later. Suddenly, we had a new family that folded us in their arms. Older Christians became like mothers and fathers; younger couples welcomed us as brothers and sisters. As they invited us to traipse up a snowy mountain looking for a Christmas tree with our kids, or go weekend camping, or help a friend move, or spend an afternoon fishing, we bonded through shared lives. One woman asked me to help serve lunch to inner city kids at the mission downtown. Others invited our kids to playgroups, and us to a Bible study. Sometimes we laughed out of control, or cried together. We even stood in the rain to pray together. This was family love, the kind I had barely felt before. And it made me homesick for more.

I learned one startling thing. Perhaps two. The first was that authentic Christians exude the aroma of God's family love without trying. Familiar, yet hard to place at first, it's an aroma like company's coming, family fun, acceptance, mercy, and love all rolled into one. It smells of everything good and lovely, of freedom to grow, delicious warmth and laughter, music and beauty, grace and forgiveness.

But part of the aroma is foreign to my senses, otherworldly. It's something I know little of, but am powerfully drawn to. It smells like sacrifice. It can only be the smell of heaven.

The first time I caught the scent, I was sick in bed with bronchitis. Lauren was three, climbing all over me on the couch trying to entertain me with stories, songs, and coloring books. Steve was in California at a weeklong conference. When we spoke on the phone, I covered up how ill I really was. Neither did I tell my neighbors or church family. Instead, I grew sicker by the day, barely able to get up and make meals for Lauren and me. When I finally went to a doctor, I was close to pneumonia. *Surely an antibiotic will fix me up*, I thought.

Not so.

I vaguely remember hearing the phone ring one morning, sounding like it came from a long corridor. I opened my eyes and glanced around the living room. Lauren was nowhere in sight. Dragging myself to the kitchen phone, I answered in a raspy voice.

"Virelle, where have you been?" It was Sue, our pastor's wife. "No one's seen or heard from you in a couple of weeks."

"Well, I've been . . . " A violent coughing spell finished my sentence. When I reached for a glass of water, suddenly the room swirled. *Oh, my head!* I slid to the floor.

Sue called to me from the dangling phone cord. "Virelle? Can you hear me? I'm coming over. Unlock the front door and get in bed." But I felt too weak to climb the stairs and headed back to the couch. *Where was Lauren? Oh, God, I need help.*

In a half hour, Sue was on my front porch, bags of groceries in her arms. Lauren, who'd been coloring in her room the whole time, ran downstairs still in her pajamas and let Sue in with a big hug. *Poor kid's been neglected with me so sick!* I noticed her hair still stuck out in yesterday's ponytails. *Oh, what a bad mother I am!*

"Okay, honey, let's get you dressed," Sue said cheerfully. "I'll fix lunch for you and Mommy, then you're coming home with me to play with our girls. How's that?"

That was good. Very good indeed. Lauren leaped back upstairs to pick out something to wear.

Next, Sue looked at my pathetic face and stringy hair peeking out from under an old quilt. Her voice was firm but kind when she said, "You never should have kept quiet when you were so sick, Virelle.

Especially with Steve out of town. Don't you know we'd all want to help you and pray for you?"

I didn't.

"Don't do that again, okay?"

I wouldn't. I shook my head, unleashing another violent coughing spell.

"I'll heat up some chicken soup for you. I made sandwiches. I think I'd better air out the house, too." *Maybe we should just blow it up instead,* I thought.

For the next few days, a parade of saints brought meals to our house every night, and escorted Lauren to play with a variety of friends so I could rest. Steve soon came home and took over my care, the house, and laundry. Recovery took longer than I'd imagined, which might have been due to a stunning surprise we soon learned about—our longed-for Baby Number Two was on the way!

To be honest, experiencing such sacrificial service made me regard God's family and our one-day home in heaven in vivid, real terms, like sniffing an aroma from someplace I'd once loved, such as my Aunt Char's kitchen. It made me want to give back to God. But what could I give? I had so little to offer. Until one day it occurred to me, I could just give myself—climb on the altar willingly. *Take me, Lord. Take anything You want. I'm Yours!*

It didn't sound like much. I had a body with relative health and energy. I could cook and clean, tell stories, bring a smile. Maybe God could use something like that.

Yes, in fact, He could. All the time.

God visited me with unexpected joy at each small sacrifice. Whether getting up with kids during the night, or packing Steve's suitcase one more time, or cooking meals big enough to share with a neighbor, I found strange new delights doing ordinary things with the idea of offering them back to God. Somehow, I knew He received them with pleasure. Imagine that!

I had much to learn. Having always thrived on approval and outward expressions of thanks, after a while I didn't do too well when only God noticed my little acts of service. Naturally, God used His own children to "grow me up" by example. He sent my friend Judy, a missionary home on furlough from Taiwan, someone whose life always seemed glamorously filled with God's appointments. Mine was pretty plain in comparison.

One day, Judy left our home after she and her four kids had come for lunch. As always, her flair for honesty and directness bolstered my soul in ways that lingered long afterward. As she stepped out the front door, she paused a moment and reflected, "I've begun to see everything I do now as a ministry. It doesn't matter what it is. That gets me excited to get up every day."

Waving good-bye, I heard a small whisper to my heart. *Would that be enough for you, Virelle?*

What, Lord? Do You mean view my life full of ministry like hers? But it isn't.

Who says?

Hm-m-m. How do I do that?

No matter what I give you, just do it for Me. Climb up on the altar and sing, Child. I'll hear it. You can depend on it.

I guessed I could do that. A little at a time, perhaps, but I could learn to do that.

That was many years ago. Judy was right. Honestly, I still like to be thanked. But the secret joy of offering even small acts of service to God, just for Him alone even if no one else appreciates it, really is unequalled, flat out hard to beat.

The problem is, every sacrifice needs an altar, but altars aren't easy places. Some of mine was cleaning my elderly mother's refrigerator when it was ready to walk away on its own (*Lord, this is making me gag!*); or stepping into the studio with terror in my heart to host my first radio show (*Couldn't You find someone better to do this?*); or caring for my husband after his open-heart surgery (*I'm so not the "nursey" type.*). It shames me to speak of my struggles over such small sacrifices, really, when compared to the huge things others have done.

Altars mean death. Climbing up there is the final countdown to the death of my own way, especially my dreams for those I love. That hurts.

A dear former pastor Peter Letchford once encouraged me, saying, "My experience has been that God only leads us to Gethsemane once. What He seems after is our willingness to follow Him there no matter what the cost." The relief was enormous. Only once. I hadn't thought of it like that. Jesus went once to Gethsemane. God would not require more of me, either.

Oh, God, thank You! Thank You for allowing me altars and sacrifices to learn to climb. Walk with me through my Gethsemane, when it comes, and give me Your comfort there, and Your aroma for someone else.

CHAPTER 16

Finding My Song

I never planned on being a writer. I literally fell into it one brilliant June morning in front of the Red Lion Inn in Stockbridge, Massachusetts. Besides embarrassing me, falling also hurt. I picked myself up from the sidewalk and looked down at my knees. No blood. Amazing! Stopped midstreet behind me were my father-in-law and our Guatemalan exchange student, Alejandra, bent in half with laughter.

"You looked so hilarious when you did that!" They slapped their knees and pointed at me, showing no self-control at all.

"It's not funny." My mother-in-law helped me up and chided them in her low, sweet voice, but no one was listening. Aching with laughter, they could barely walk a straight line across the street. No bones felt broken. I determined to throw my foolish new high heels away as soon as I got home.

A few hours later, after we lunched at the inn's grand dining room and wandered through the quaint shops in Norman Rockwell's hometown, we piled into the car to head home. Something felt odd and out of kilter in my neck and back. *I wonder what that is?*

I found out soon enough. Within days I was limping slightly on walks around the block and experiencing numbness in my left arm and hand. X-rays and tests confirmed the diagnosis: two slipped discs in my neck and lower back that required months of neck traction and a cervical collar. Not welcome news for this mom in high gear.

Fifteen months of pain and limited activity followed, dwindling down to mostly one activity: sitting behind our bedroom door with my head in a harness on one side and a pulley system with weights on the other. In this fixed state I sat for two hours daily. My head tipped forward in a sadistic noose, all I could manage now was reading. While I was thinking the obvious—*Maybe I'd better read my Bible*—it literally fell open to Jesus' words in Matthew chapter 11: "Come to me, all you who are weary and burdened, and I will give you rest. Take my yoke upon you; and learn from me . . . For my yoke is easy, and my burden is light" (vv. 28–30). Why was I surprised?

Wait a minute. This is Your yoke I'm wearing, Lord? This isn't feeling easy.

" . . . and learn of me," *I do have a lot to learn.*

" . . . for my yoke is eas,y and my burden is light." *Easy? Light? How can that be unless . . . unless You carry the heavy end?*

"Of course."

There was little choice but to settle into my new contraption and learn to listen to God all over again. It took time to adjust, but after a few weeks, meeting Him alone behind my bedroom door became the perfect escape. I'd slip on my "noose" and sit quietly (*How funny! I couldn't even move my jaw!*), reading His Word. Listening. Resting there. Within a few months, the strangest thing would happen.

Something like a song begging a voice echoed from a place before unknown. Day by day, it drifted through forgotten rooms in my soul where faces and voices I'd once loved still lived. I longed to bring them to life again, to listen and linger over ideas once muffled by my busy life.

What am I to do with this?

"Tell someone."

I'll tell Steve.

And so, added to our ritual mug of morning coffee while Steve shaved in the bathroom, the song found a voice as I shared my unearthed memories. His interest surprised me. He'd hum approval as he whisked his razor through the white foam. "Tell me more." He'd nod. "What happened then?" One morning he put the razor down, bent to rinse and dry his face slowly, looked at me and said, "You have to write these stories down. Our children need them. Others need them."

"Write them? You mean like for our kids?"

"Yes, but not just for our kids. Why not a book?"

"Oh, no! I'm not that good!"

"Yes, you are. How do you know until you try?"

Hadn't we said the same thing to our kids? I was cornered. "Okay. I'll try."

Around that same time, the New York State Writer's Institute ran a brief newspaper ad announcing a six-week course on Wednesday evenings for beginning writers. A local children's author, Athena Lord, was teaching it at our town library. Why not go? Mr. Encouragement agreed to go with me.

He went once. Business travel soon filled up Steve's Wednesdays, so I went alone. Six or eight people came, from twenty-somethings to retired folks, each with varied backgrounds and experience. Every week we were to write something and share it with the group. Stories that had camped in my brain for months found life on a yellow legal pad.

In the second class, when it was my turn, I read nervously. The circle of writers said nothing. They just sat. *They must hate it!* I wanted to slither away quietly.

"You need to do something with this," Athena said. "See me afterward."

Like what? Burn it?

I listened for the next forty-five minutes as others read their work, some compelling, others less so. Each one received positive comments and constructive criticism from the group. Everyone but me. After they all left, I stood by a bookshelf waiting for Athena to finish stuffing papers into her briefcase. She finally looked up and asked, "What did you say your name was?"

"Virelle. Virelle Kidder."

"Oh, yes. Unusual name. Virelle, you need to write for publication. Your work is good. Still needs revision, of course, but I want you to consider submitting it."

"Submitting it? I'm not sure I can. I mean, I don't know how to do that."

"I'll show you how. Just keep writing."

I promised her I would and stammered my thanks, but driving home later in the chilly darkness, I thought it was an impossibility. *How could I do that? I'm just a mom with a houseful of kids.* But I couldn't wait to tell Steve on the phone that night what had happened.

Without knowing another Christian writer, I began writing more stories, reading my drafts to Steve in the morning while he shaved. He often took them to work to his friend Paul Hayford, a brilliant PhD in English literature who was also a Christian. Paul would edit them; when they came back to me a month later, they'd look like a Christmas tree trimmed in red ink. In a primitive effort at submission, I sent my writing out once in a while, collecting six rejections in two years. I was crushed.

One day my friend Ruth Camp called to suggest I send some chapters to her husband's golfing buddy, who had just retired as editor of Victor Books. In an act of mercy, he sent them to Carole Sanderson Streeter, an acquisitions editor at Victor, who called one day asking if she could stop by en route home from Boston.

"Absolutely! Come stay with us!" *What am I saying? This is a big editor from Chicago!*

It amazes me that she agreed to come, but she happily accepted my invitation, as though she did this every day. Miracle of miracles, the pot roast and vegetables came out perfect, and the kids were angels. *Thank You, Lord!* Carole appeared to enjoy herself a lot. Steve kept a roaring fire going in the woodstove while we chatted about her life and ours until we went to bed.

The following morning after breakfast, Carole and I went for a walk, then sat again in the family room over one last cup of coffee. But nothing was happening as I'd hoped. Not even a word of interest. *Lord, she's leaving in a few minutes and hasn't even mentioned my writing once!* I felt confused and discouraged. As I rose to carry our coffee cups to the kitchen, Carole asked a question I'll never forget.

"If you had only one thing to write about in the next ten years, what would it be?"

"In the next ten years?" *Only one thing? Rats! I wanted to write about lots of things.* I thought quietly a moment. What *did* matter to me most? I knew instantly.

"I'd write about being a mom."

"That's what I thought. I'd like to have your ideas for that on my desk as soon as possible. Then we'll talk some more." With that said, Carole hugged me and left.

That was November. On Christmas Eve I sat late by the Christmas tree with a yellow legal pad on my lap. Everything was wrapped and done. The kids were in bed, and I'd promised Steve I'd be upstairs in a minute, too. *What did matter most to me about being a mom? A lot.* In forty-five minutes, I made a list of my struggles, and how God had helped me through them over the previous eighteen years. The day after Christmas, having passed through our coffee-in-the-bathroom test, I typed it up and sent it to Carole.

She called immediately. "I love it! Now, put it in proposal form and send it to me again."

"What's that?"

Carole explained a proposal, something to which whole books are devoted, in the next five minutes. I was off and running. Within a month, I'd sent her an official proposal, which led to my first book contract the following month. Thanks to Paul Hayford, Ruth Camp, Carole Streeter at Victor Books, and especially Steve and our kids, *Mothering Upstream*, was eventually published.

Writing became my song to sing back to God. Although my writing springs from the personal stories and real people that camp in my memory, it's mostly about who God is, not who I am.

There are still times when I lose my tune. When I haven't been still enough to listen, the melody waits for me to sit quietly again. And Jesus walks through my soul, fingering my memory, awakening a new song that's all about His love.

CHAPTER 17

Daddy Comfort

It's hard to imagine anything more wonderful than being hugged. You can't buy a sincere hug anywhere. It's priceless. Neither my brother Roger nor I can remember my father hugging us when we were small, but he probably did. My mother gave hugs, but was uncomfortable with open displays of affection or talking about feelings. Anger wasn't done; neither were any emotions other than laughter.

The Kidders were different. A huge family with Swedish, English, and French roots, what they lacked in money was banked in the elevated importance of fun, faith, and love. They didn't hide emotion, nor did they embellish it. They just lived it. Marrying into Steve's family was the best thing I ever did, but a culture shock just the same. For one thing, there were so many of them. Not only did Steve have five brothers and sisters, but so did his dad. Every branch of the family traced its roots to early setters in the Chautauqua county region, and abounded with brothers and sisters, aunts, uncles, and cousins who loved God and who loved being together.

Every summer the Kidder clan gathered at Long Point State Park on Chautauqua Lake for an all-day family reunion. It always began by holding hands in a circle and singing the doxology. Invariably, several people cried, remembering how Grandma Kidder began the tradition two generations ago. Next came a hearty invitation to tables of home-made food, profuse compliments, lots of loud laughter, and kids giggling. Aunts, uncles, and cousins gathered their chairs in a circle to hear this season's fishing and hunting stories, share great conversations about local politics and church news, and pass around photos with updates on all the family. After an enormous meal, someone usually organized a water balloon toss for the kids, a game of touch football or softball, and of course, fishing and swimming. Picnics, in Steve's family, were the backdrop in his album of memories. Photos abound of cousins in swimsuits, aunts and uncles enjoying one another, new babies being passed around and adored. And hugs. Always hugs.

It was new to me in lots of ways, like hearing total freedom of expression, even from children, saying things like, "It's not fair she doesn't have the same rules I had at that age," or "Can I have a party here for my friend's birthday?" or "Sorry. We can't afford that now. Maybe next time." No one was afraid to speak his or her mind, within certain limits.

I figured Grandma Kidder did it. Someone must have set the rules long ago, like no whining, no sassing. No means no, and a promise is a promise. Every branch of the family insisted on kindness and courtesy to everyone. Displaying rudeness and bad manners was asking for trouble. In Steve's house, mealtimes began with prayer together. That also meant show up on time, no ball caps at the table, wait your turn and ask nicely, listen when others are talking, and always express appreciation for Mom's great cooking. Everyone took turns doing dishes. It was only fair. I liked it.

In fact, I liked it all, especially the positive intensity my new family brought to living. Somehow, it felt right. Authentic. Healthy. It was obvious; to me Steve's family loved being together. And still do.

I longed to feel part of that family. It took me awhile to realize I actually was. Part of me held back. Could I adjust to a family that had a dad, a loving and expressive, grounded and steady one like Steve's? One who wouldn't fly off the handle, or leave; one you could relax and talk with?

Growing up without a dad leaves gaping holes in a child's heart. My father's absence left me hungry for a father's love, but afraid of it just the same. Among the many things I loved about Steve right from the start were his steadiness, reliability, honesty, kindness, and gentlemanly ways. He was also the most fun and interesting guy I'd ever met. It wasn't until I got to know his dad that I figured out why he was like that. He was just like him.

Having seldom seen married people up close, I watched his parents closely, impressed with the great respect they showed each other. Their love was obvious but natural. Both were cheerful and uncomplaining, hardworking and appreciative of one another. "He's not a perfect man," my mother-in-law confided recently, "but he's the best man I've ever known." They made home a safe place. Mom and Dad were predictable, reasonable, and didn't embarrass their children. Instead, they welcomed others into their large family circle.

Their eldest son, Bruce, had a close high school buddy who lived in poverty. Due to some extreme difficulties, he needed another place to live. One day Bruce asked, "Can Chuck live with us? He has nowhere to go." The house was already full with six kids and only one bathroom. Mom and Dad shared a quiet glance that Bruce understood. "He can have my room," he said. "We can take turns sleeping on the couch."

Thus it was decided. No one complained or argued about the relative inconvenience. Chuck became a member of Steve's family his last few years in high school, growing to love his parents as he would his own. Eventually, he earned a doctorate and achieved national recognition in his field of study, often bringing his own family back for annual reunions. His story marked every child in that home, as did his death just one year ago.

What amazed me most was that Bruce even asked. In a family with six children living on a modest income in a small frame house, where his dad often worked more than one job to feed the family, why was Bruce not afraid to ask? Most parents would have laughed at such a request to add one more mouth to feed, and six more shirts to iron every week. But Bruce knew his parents valued children and families over everything. They knew how important it was for kids to sleep peacefully at night, have a meal on the table, and enjoy harmony in the home.

Faith in God mattered a lot. Even though he wasn't strongly evangelical, Steve's dad insisted that everyone under his roof attend church and Sunday school regularly. It wasn't optional. Neither was good behavior in church. He'd pass Life Savers down the pew to reward good behavior, and give "the fish eye" to wigglers. Discipline was fair and meaningful, and not overdone. Using bad language, especially misusing the Lord's name, was never allowed. Neither was being disrespectful to Mom. It was a line no one challenged.

None of those six kids turned out perfect. I know. I married one of them. But they carried into life a deep sense of being loved, accepted, and highly valued. Each one is enormously dependable, a capable hard worker in a wide variety of professions. Celebrating family is on the top of their priority list, and service to others close behind it. And our kids love every one of them. A recent event framed it well.

Last summer, our older son, David, on a trip to western New York with his wife and new baby, Jack, arranged for a four-generation photo to be taken with his dad, grandpa, and Jack. It was a rare moment. Steve and his dad still look like clones born thirty years apart. They sat with Jack on Grandpa's lap and Dave's arm around both men he loves so much. Lauren and Michael and their family, as well some of Steve's brothers and sisters were there for family pictures, too.

Looking at the framed photo on my wall, I asked myself today, what made this family special? Why do the children, now well into adult life, and troops of grandchildren and great-grandchildren, gather so much strength, wisdom, and comfort from their parents, now ninety-one and ninety-four years old?

It has to be love. Unconditional, free, grace-filled parental love. It's the closest match for God's love in this world and leads a child to want more. Only God's love fills the deepest void of the human soul, regardless of our family of origin. But a father's embrace is unique and powerful. It can win a child's heart early and last a lifetime.

When Steve had his heart attack last winter, I called his parents daily to give them updates, knowing it was impossible for them to travel to Florida to see him. His dad often choked up when he said, "I just wish I could give him a hug."

Mom always added, "Tell him we love him." Even in ICU, hearing that gave Steve comfort.

I couldn't wait until he was well and we could walk through Mom and Dad's front door again. It finally happened last month, when Steve and I traveled to New York for an extended visit, over a year since those family pictures. Both Mom and Dad met us at the door, as they always had, with smiles and arms outstretched. He hugged them both, but his dad held on to Steve a long time and wept. "I just wanted to give you a hug," he said, tears rolling down his cheeks. Then he and Mom looked at me, and said, "Thank you for taking such good care of him.

Thank you for doing your best to make this happen." I never expected it. I cried, too.

I pray everyone in our family knows the same love. Today, Steve and I see our chief function in the family as prayer warriors, not advice givers, as tempting as that often is. I'm convinced few family problems cannot be solved with big doses of prayer, laughter, listening, and hugs. Always hugs.

CHAPTER 18

New Dreams

It's almost New Year's Day, one of our favorite days of the year. Ask anyone who's ever invited us to attend an event on January first. We always turn them down nicely. "Sorry. Can't come. We have plans that day."

Often they ask, "What are you doing?"

Then we have to tell the truth. "We spend the day together dreaming and planning for the new year." Admittedly, it sounds weird, but neither of us would miss one of our favorite rituals.

When we lived in New York, Steve began our morning with a fire in the woodstove. At our condo in Florida, we open the patio doors and let the breeze blow through the house, crank up the music, and prepare to do little or nothing all day but talk, eat, pray, and go for a walk on the beach.

First comes freshly ground coffee, and lots of it. You can't separate a Swede from his coffee. Next, we make a big hot breakfast together, usually huge fluffy pancakes, family favorites we call Grandpa's Buttermilk

Beauties dripping with butter and real maple syrup. Add a little lean ham and fresh orange juice, and a "food coma" is on the way. Steve has no restraint. He can handle six huge ones shamelessly. Then comes the best part.

"Are you ready?" he asks, settling into the couch with his Bible and personal notebook open.

"Ready." I join him with two fresh cups of coffee, and my Bible and notebook, too. Sitting together, we begin every new year holding hands in prayer, taking turns thanking God for His amazing grace and goodness to us in the previous year. Sometimes I review the answered prayer requests recorded in my notebook. Not every one does, but most have a date in the margin indicating the way God answered. Another cup of coffee to celebrate.

Gratefulness over answered prayer gives us confidence to bring anything to God, any need at all, and know it will be heard. Together we expand our family prayer list to include others with huge health needs, our church and missionaries, friends and relatives who have yet to come to faith. All sorts of things. I know God will answer each one in His perfect way.

"Okay, now let's look at last year's dreams and goals and see how we did. Brace yourself!" We both open to a private page with five to ten dreams and goals each, listed last New Year's Day. Steve's the bravest. He reads his list first. "Take another course in stone carving . . . did bronze casting instead of that. Learn to sail better . . . well, I guess we're learning. Run five miles a day . . . I wonder when I can do that again? How about you?"

"Lose fifteen pounds . . . yup! Did that for the first time in years."

"I lost more than I planned," Steve said.

"You did do that. Now let's see. Be faithful at tennis . . . we both did okay until December. Let's see, read through the Bible . . . nope. Only made it to September on that one. Finish writing a new book . . . almost done. Send out two proposals a year . . . not going to happen for a while."

"Anything else?"

"Yeah, spend more time with kids and grandkids, but how are we going to do that now?"

We both grew quiet again. This year was like no other. Not only had we, by some miracle, relocated to Florida but we now lived within minutes of two amazing heart centers just in time for Steve's major heart attack only three weeks earlier. Only God could have arranged that level of care so close to us.

Tears came quickly. "I wondered if we'd ever do this again. Now here we are." Steve put his arms around me and held me as I cried. Death had come close, to be sure. Two stents and an angioplasty fixed only half his heart. A triple bypass was a month away. What would life be like then?

He kissed the top of my head. We held each other a long time.

"There's no guarantee we'll even be here next year, is there?" I sniffled.

"No. Every year's a gift."

"I love you so."

"I love you, too."

Writing now about such a private moment brings tears again.

May I tell you what we wrote for our dreams and goals this year? Let me find the page. Here it is:

- Listen more closely to God
- Make it through the year without dialing 911
- Learn to sail our little boat better
- Save more, give more

- Make a strong recovery, doing everything to make that happen
- Deal with letting go of plans
- Have more fun together than ever before
- Celebrate each new day
- (me) Finish another new book, if God allows
- Write a bestseller (still a dream!)
- Find new ways to love our kids and grandkids from a distance

As the one-year anniversary of Steve's heart attack approaches this year on December ninth, I realize how closely we've hit the mark on many of these dreams and goals. For one, they are all very simple now. And every one includes looking God in the face, and stepping into each new day with one resolve: pleasing Him.

What peace has come into our marriage since we began this New Year's Day celebration many years ago. We may never achieve all our personal goals like losing more weight or winning athletic awards (one of Steve's former hobbies was competing in the pentathlon in the Senior Games in New York), but what we get to keep is priceless: running our earthly race for His pleasure. Nothing better.

It's easy to lose sight of that and get distracted by responsibilities, worries, and small setbacks. This week I overheard my thoughts and they sound like the whining of a toddler. "Lord, I'm tired of writing these stories. They're too much about me. I want to write something easier, more fun. Aren't you done having me write about my life yet?"

Do you want to stop, Virelle? The Spirit of God edged closer and whispered softly.

"No. I just want to write something more fun. I'm tired of this."

Are you tired of serving Me? The question brought me up short.

"Oh, no! That's not what I meant at all, Lord."

Do you want Me to replace you?

"Oh, no! That's not what I meant either. I just meant . . . "

The time will come, Virelle, when this will end. I will have new things for you to do. Until then, are you willing to continue writing for Me?

Yes, Lord. . . . What a worm I've been! Father, forgive me for wanting my own way again. Direct me any way You wish. I'm happy just serving You, Lord.

Now I realize God edits my list of dreams and goals, even my prayers, to fit His will. When I'm off base, He redirects and grants what is best for me. Even a "No" answer is a good one. Had we judiciously planned our own way several years ago, remaining in Albany longer, Steve might not be alive now. When God said, "Go!" we moved fast even if it looked wildly crazy at the time.

There was a time when I didn't dare to dream new dreams, feeling fairly certain they'd never happen. Dreams were for people with too much time, without their feet on the ground. How wrong I was!

As we read together two of John Eldredge's books, *The Sacred Romance* and *Journey of Desire*, God gave life to dreams we once thought impossible, such as living in a warmer climate, learning to sail, taking up a sport, and traveling more. Today we are living out many of them. There are more to come, dreams for greater effectiveness in writing and speaking; for ministry beyond our borders; mind-blowing, spirit-expanding dreams that grow us up to do God's wonderful will.

Here's the kicker: They are all God's secrets until the day He plants them in our heart. Usher in wonder, joy, amazement, and hard work. Life will never be the same again.

I love splashing encouragement and belief on other people's dreams. Especially on new writers. As a mentor at the Jerry B. Jenkins Christian Writer's Guild, I get to do that every day as I review students' lessons and help them improve. Sometimes God helps me spot a new novelist, or a gifted journalist. A few of my students are now full-time professional writers. I love helping them fine-tune their skills and fan their dreams into reality.

Others I've met have enormous ability and training, but need someone to give them a push—call it a divine shove—to accomplish more. For some strange reason, God has allowed me to tap a few on the shoulder, or make introductions, that led to bestselling books.

How does that happen? I have no special gift but one, and it's not really a gift at all. It's a privilege everyone is offered, but few accept: the joy of walking with Jesus every day. Simple as that. He leads, I follow. When I mess things up, and I do, He stops me gently, looks me in the eyes, and says, *Do you want to continue in My will,* Child?

"Yes, Lord."

Then follow Me. His voice is kind, like a verbal embrace. I remember John's words, so like Jesus' own, when he wrote, "Dear friends, if our hearts do not condemn us, we have confidence before God and receive from him anything we ask, because we obey his commands and do what pleases him. And this is his command: to believe in the name of his Son, Jesus Christ, and to love one another as he commanded us" (1 John 3:21–23).

In this new year and every one to come, nothing matters more.

CHAPTER 19

Treasures of Grace

"I 'll see you again soon, Mother," I assured her with a smile and a hug. "It won't be long. I'll call when I get home." I turned and waved several times while waiting for the world's slowest elevator to arrive.

"Good-bye, honey. I love you." Mother, stooping feebly on her walker, waved good-bye, blonde hair framing her face as it has for many years.

"Love you, too." *Why am I so sad? We had a great visit.* The nurses say we look alike, a comment that would have made me cringe a few years ago. Not anymore. Mother's move to the nursing home delivered more than relief. It gave me freedom to celebrate all the good things she gave both Roger and me. Different from some families, but good just the same. As the elevator doors closed, Mother had already turned back toward her room. *Lord, will I see her again? Could this be it?*

In spite of her ongoing complaints about moving, these have been Mother's happiest years since she entered Alzheimer's hall of mirrors.

She is safe now, clean, consistently well cared for, and lives in an up-beat community complete with birthday parties, sing-alongs, barbeques in the gazebo, even "neighborhood" dogs who visit for their biscuit daily. Her one-room apartment reflects her treasured home in many ways, but is never quite the real thing, something she's often still bitter about.

But now Mother has Bill, the love of her elder years, and quite possibly her life. Too bad they didn't have sixty years together. Bill, with his sweeping gentlemanly gestures and a fresh flower in his lapel daily, escorts her to meals and activities, and to the restaurant downstairs for ice cream every day at two o'clock. God's brought unexpected peace to us both. With His help, I've learned to love Mother as she is, something that took me far too long.

Letting go is never easy. Chapters in life, like good-byes, are a small death to things we once thought permanent, like our kids being nearby, and our parents remaining strong and independent. This year, our parents have achieved the grand ages of ninety-four for both my mom and Steve's dad, and almost ninety-two for his mom. After each visit, we hold the treasures they've given with more reverence than we did in younger years.

Though it's uncommon in today's self-driven world, our parents consistently gave the best of themselves to their children. It's a rare legacy. In varied measures, they poured out faithful living, deep commitment, unconditional love, financial sacrifice, wisdom and forgiveness, hospitality and warmth, laughter and shared tears.

I wonder. *What treasures will we leave our kids? Is it presumptuous to ponder?* After Steve's heart attack, maybe not.

Our kids almost worship their dad. When he retired from the state education department, our family held a private party for him at a beautiful nearby restaurant. After dinner, we presented him with a leather-bound book that contained personal messages of appreciation, memories, and love. As we passed the book around the table, we each read our portion aloud amidst laughter and tears. Amy and I made Steve a ceramic clock that each family member inscribed.

Steve has rock star status, partly because the real fabric of our lives has a rougher feel. We've had plenty of ups and downs, like others. At times, I wondered if we'd survive. After all that's happened, what will our kids find worth keeping?

I hope they can find forgiveness for their parents' many flaws earlier than I did for mine. I wasted years feeling hurt over irreversible sorrows from my childhood. I'm thankful that our kids had an easier life. Still, we were fairly young believers as parents and made plenty of mistakes. Too bad we had to learn on our children.

I hope they remember laughter in our home, often out of control on my part. For example, I like to sing fake opera just to make the kids laugh, something that's become my trademark with our grandkids.

"Why are you always so silly, Nana?" my eight-year-old grandson Thane asked me, looking up from his homework after my brief aria at the kitchen sink. The question startled me back to seriousness.

"Hm-m-m. I guess it's because I choose joy, honey. There are plenty of things in the world to make us sad, don't you think?"

He thought a minute. "Yeah."

"I'm not always silly, am I, Thane?" I worried now. *Does he think I'm a complete nut?*

"No, but more than most people." *Probably true.*

"Should I try to stop? Not sure I can now."

"Uh-uh. I like you the way you are."

"Oh, good. That's how I feel about you, too."

Just as I am prone to being loud and silly, Steve has always been quiet but funny. I hope they remember his leap over the sofa one morning when all Lauren's sleepover friends sat barely awake at our kitchen table, chins drooped over their morning pancakes. "Why are they so quiet?" Steve whispered to me while I flipped more pancakes.

Seconds later, he cranked up some loud music and shouted, "Watch this, girls!" only to discover midair that the girls had moved our coffee table to the other side of the sofa. They looked up and gasped in horror, when miraculously Steve cleared both the table and the sofa. The applause was deafening, not to mention his instant heroism. I hope our kids remember things like that and more.

I'm such a chicken; I used to leave long before Steve's Star Wars games began on occasional Friday nights. Steve, wearing a stocking mask and his dark bathrobe, would hide as Darth Vader. Each of the kids, equipped with X-wing fighters or the Millennium Falcon, zoomed and flashed around the darkened house searching for him, squealing in terror and delight when, hissing and growling, he'd leap out of the laundry cabinet or mudroom closet. Sheer terror reigned.

I guess a little fake opera wasn't that bad, after all.

I know our kids will remember stories read on the couch, piggyback rides to bed, and prayer anytime, not just at meals and bedtime. I hope they remember learning to share the workload at home, changing sheets, dusting, raking leaves, stacking wood in the fall, vacuuming once in a while, and helping with dishes. I hope they remember the many others who joined our table and often, our family circle. No doubt, they will also remember discipline, spankings for big offenses when they were small, or groundings as they got older. What I hope they forget were the times I lost my temper or punished someone unfairly. What they will never know was the awful sense of failure Steve and I both felt when we had to lower the boom. Forgiveness, grace, and prayer glued us together with the Lord, who never left us for a moment.

Will they be merciful? I hope so. Will they harbor resentment over hurts? I pray not. Will they know their parents as real people, flawed but honest in their faith walk, who guided them with prayer and often tears? I believe they will. Our kids love us still (amazing grace!), and today are our best friends. That's a gift we treasure daily.

We are equals in every way, except one. Our children have become our heroes as each rose to face challenges in life Steve and I would have prevented. After many physical trials, Lauren has persevered and even prospered with lupus. Now a mom to three great kids, she and her husband, Michael, have a ministry to other young couples in their church. At this moment she's living out a dream to run her first half-marathon in January. We can hardly believe it.

Amy, having suffered with bipolar illness more than half her life, has experienced two painful divorces, and is now living on her own and working part-time. Although it's hard for her to move forward alone, she's felt tons of support from friends and family, is meeting her challenges daily, and is living with wisdom and faith. Lately, Amy's dusting off her dreams and asking God's direction for her next steps.

After college, David learned to live with very little while building a business in New York. Following a dramatic conversion experience, he's now married his perfect counterpart, José, a successful business-woman. He's become a successful entrepreneur, and has coauthored two books on the New York Times bestsellers list. They have two small sons, two big Labs, and usually a houseful of guests.

Bob overcame painful adoption issues, and many personal sorrows attached to it, to graduate tops in his field of mechanics, but even more important, he is building a family legacy as a husband and father of three amazing boys. He and his wife, Theresa, demonstrate love and graciousness in many ways, particularly this year as a close friend battled cancer.

When tried by fire, who can measure the generational effects of family love and faith? No one can, especially when it's happening. But the effects last a long time, past walkers and nursing homes, memory loss and failed vision. Past illness, prodigals, financial reversals, and even success. Legacies are built on the treasures we received from our parents, and carry into our own lives. Some are too precious for words.

On our last visit to see Steve's folks, as on every visit, we sat at breakfast over sweet rolls and coffee, enjoying the birds and squirrels beyond the patio doors. Steve's mom quietly drifted down the hall for a moment. She moves like a mouse.

"Just fed 'em," his dad said, wiping the chill from his nose with a tissue. "Watch that little chipmunk. He'll come right from behind the planter to pick up that extra seed I leave for him." He chuckled like he'd trained it.

"So are you going hunting this year, Dad?" Steve asked.

"Oh, I might. We'll see how the weather is." Even at ninety-four, he'd seldom missed opening day in years. It was the memory that mattered, celebrating sunrise together in the woods with two of his sons. Dad would pack egg salad sandwiches, Mom's refrigerator cookies, and a thermos of coffee for each one, an annual ritual. Who knew? This might be the year for another big buck, like the two he and Steve bagged one year. He never gave up.

Just then, Mom returned to the kitchen, brushing silently past the back of Steve's chair. Her warm, soft hands caressed his cheek as she bent down to plant a little kiss on her favorite spot on the back of his neck. "My favorite son," she whispered. Steve ate it up. It didn't matter that Mom said that to all her sons and daughters. At that moment, he was, indeed, her favorite and he knew it.

Is it any wonder why their six children still return home at every opportunity to see Mom and Dad? Their embrace includes me, too, a grace that warms me to my toes.

"Who wants more coffee?" I ask, already moving toward the coffee-maker. "I'll make another pot." Anything to make the morning last longer.

CHAPTER 20

Every New Morning

It's the strangest thing about growing older; even as I write this, songs I learned at summer camp and vacation Bible school rise in my heart each day. "Welcome Happy Morning, Rise and Shine to Thee!" "This Little Light of Mine, I'm Going to Let It Shine!" "I've got that joy, joy, joy, joy down in my heart. Where? down in my heart to stay!" When I forget the words, I make them up, just like I did then. Favorite old hymns blend with newer worship songs and fill my mind when I'm not looking. And I'm not alone. Steve finds himself humming the doxology all day long. It could be the best part about our senior years!

Worship sweeps through my heart now, frivolously unplanned and free. I feel deeper love for my husband, children, and grandchildren, and gratefulness to God for all He's given, and strangely, for what He's not given. Even when bad news threatens to rattle me again, it's easier now to run to God and give Him my problems, certain He will do what's best.

Sometimes, fearing it won't last, I turn to Jesus and ask, *How come, Lord? Why do I have this joy? I'm not special. I'm very ordinary, just a kid from a little red house in upstate New York who talked to You in the woods.*

Ah, yes.

How well I remember that young girl with scraggly blonde hair in a ponytail, wearing a red cowgirl hat, six-shooters, and cowboy boots. Often I grabbed berry baskets from the barn and headed out to pick blackberries in my beloved woods behind our house. After I passed the weeds and brambles, and stomped through last year's piled leaves, a sun-dappled sanctuary opened, canopied with tree branches and vines. The winding path, known only to me and my girlfriend Barbie, twisted behind the old Victorian homes on Spring Street and bent to the left, past the sounds of voices and lawn mowers. Only one short stretch of pathway made me nervous, where it backed up to a vacant old house rumored to have ghosts. I walked faster there, turning my face away from its overgrown backyard.

The blackberry bushes lay in a tangled mass, clothing the hill behind the Church Street houses. They protected the secret clearing Barbie and I made with its circle of rocks for our pretend campfires. After picking berries, I sat on the log benches we dragged around our "fire" and ate some, usually caught up in my own tangled thoughts about the meaning of life and our family's secrets. It was my only safe place to talk to God out loud. But He never answered back. I used to leave the woods wondering if He heard me at all, or was even real.

I was with you there, Child. I heard every word.

"Yes, Lord, You were. I'm sorry it took me so long to believe You."

I am with you now. As you follow Me, My joy is in you.

"Is that where the joy comes from? Because You are with Me?"

I am with you always.

"Our time together is sweet, Lord. I love being with You."

I will never leave you or forsake you, even to your old age.

"Thank You, Lord. Old age frightens me sometimes."

We talk like that now. There's nothing I cannot bring to Him. He's been true to His Word, to every promise, even those I feared to trust. My campfire questions have been more than answered in His Word, and in drawing close in prayer, especially when my heart was breaking. How slow I was to learn to trust Jesus fully. Life is much easier now.

In fact, if my life should end right now, or very soon, that's fine with me. Except for a deep longing to have more time with my husband, kids, and grandkids, I have nothing more I need. My soul settles quietly in His lap. Everything from now on, including outside ministry, is gravy.

Just this morning, I received word from a dear Christian sister, a fellow writer and speaker, that she was diagnosed yesterday with a large, malignant brain tumor. Her doctor and several attending nurses broke the news. Later they remarked how amazed they were at her calm response. "We've never seen anyone take this news so calmly."

Is she without hope of living? Not at all. She fully trusts God's plan to heal her with prayer, plus a rigorous plan of chemo and radiation. But if He calls her home instead? She's ready. Her life is resting quietly on the same great Lap.

There's no need for believers to run fast past the "boogeyman," the way I rushed on the wooded path past the vacant house that scared me as a child. When my days have reached completion, I know for certain Jesus will come with His head thrown back in a loving smile, and His nail-scarred hands outstretched, to walk me through heaven's ancient door unafraid and full of joy. He will do the same for all His children. We are all His "favorites."

What a privilege it has been to sit here with you and record the story of God's loving intervention in my life from earliest days until today. I marvel all over again at His patience and grace. When Moody Publishers first asked me to consider the task, I wondered, "Why would anyone want to read it?" Now I know that everyone's story is precious to God our Father, even mine, and He will direct this book to those who most need to hear it.

May you find His voice, not mine, the strongest here. May His encouragement prove true in your life as well as mine. May His invitation remain with you, to trust Jesus fully, and to rest your life fully in His care. Invite Him to own your dreams, your desires, and even your broken heart. He will not waste the tiniest bit. Rather, He will create a story that is uniquely His, and yours at the same time. He'll give you a new song to sing in the night, a love song to carry in your heart into every new morning.

A Word of Thanks

When Jennifer Lyell, my energetic and imaginative editor at Moody Publishers, asked me to consider writing a book about my life, I couldn't imagine why anyone would read it. Then, she added, "This would be a book about the ways God has intervened in your life all along the way. What have you learned from Him about the best life He has for you?"

Now, that got me excited. First, because it was a safe bet no one would ever ask me to do this again, and second, because the story of God's persistent, uncomfortable, nudging but, oh so loving, Presence all these years is a good one. In fact, I couldn't have lived without it. I'm fairly sure my kids will read this, maybe even my grandkids someday. But you, my friend, haven't heard this yet, or at least, not most of it. I pray God will fling these stories of His love, power, provision, and tenderness, into your heart.

You'll find He's clipped my wings more than a few times, required more than I ever imagined or thought possible, and allowed experiences

I'd have gladly dodged, but the reward of the narrow way is sweet. It's Jesus Himself, feeling His company, hearing His voice, leaning into Him for comfort and strength.

Were it not for Jennifer Lyell, I'd never have thought of writing this. Thank you for calling to remembrance the best and worst days of my life, and His amazing Presence there. Rhonda Elfstrand, your creativity and marketing insights are energizing. Thank you for all you've done, along with Janis Backing, Pam Pugh, and others at Moody to place this book in readers' hands.

To my agent and trusted friend Steve Laube, go my deep thanks for your creative and prayerful guidance. I look forward to what's next.

Everything I write passes through my three online writing buddies, Michele Huey, Christa Parrish, and Melanie Rigney. You are tough, insightful, and never easy on me, but I love you all for that, especially for praying and cheering me on.

No one but God knows me as well as my husband, Steve, and loves me just the same. Reading these chapters aloud to you, hearing your laughter, seeing your tears, encouraged me to the core. You are still my prince, and always will be.

To my generous and loving children, thank you for allowing me to share some of your stories, too. You are my heroes.

Most of all, thank You, heavenly Father, for surprising me on my path early, and extending Your love that never let me go.

About the Author

For over twenty-five years Virelle Kidder has been doing what she loves best—speaking to audiences around the country and abroad about the love of Christ. Virelle is a "people person" who relates instantly and warmly to audiences of all sizes. She is funny, transparent, highly relatable, and solidly biblical. A full-time writer and conference speaker, Virelle also hosted a daily radio talk show in New York's capital district. Now she's a Florida resident, still focused on encouraging women on their spiritual journey.

The Best Life Ain't Easy, But It's Worth It is Virelle's sixth book and follows on the heels of *Meet Me at the Well, Take a Month and Water Your Soul.* Both are intensely personal books, illustrating her honest, but seldom easy, walk with God. Virelle's writing has been widely published in national magazines and around the world. As a mentor for the Jerry B. Jenkins Christian Writer's Guild, she loves helping new writers learn their craft and step into their calling.

Virelle and her husband, Steve, have four grown children and eight grandchildren, who love visiting Nana and Papa in Sebastian, Florida.

You can contact Virelle, listen to her audio blog, and register for free gifts from time to time on her Web site at http//:www.virellekidder.com.

MEET ME AT THE WELL

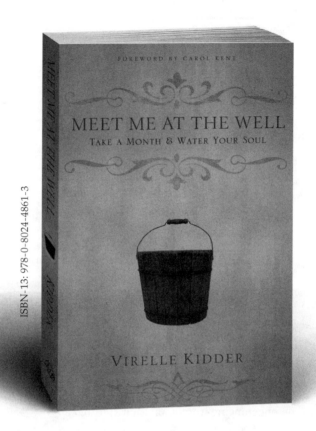

Noted speaker and author Virelle Kidder recently found herself at the end of her rope following a year of crises with her children and her mother. The end of that rope led to the well of Living Water! What started out as a drought in her life became the impetus for drawing deep. Virelle's candid, and oft-times humorous, reflection on the power of the Living Water will lead women to a month-long time of refreshment. She encourages all women to *Meet Me at the Well.*

MOODY
PUBLISHERS.

1-800-678-8812 · MOODYPUBLISHERS.COM